BASIC BIBLE DICTIONARY

by
Velda Matthews
and
Ray Beard

STANDARD
PUBLISHING
Cincinnati, Ohio

Illustrated by Richard Wahl (paintings)
and Romilda Dilley (line drawings)

Sixth Printing, 1994

Library of Congress Cataloging in Publication Data

Matthews, Velda.
  Basic Bible dictionary.

  1. Bible—dictionaries.   I. Beard, Ray.
II. Title.
BS440.M418   1984   220.3   83-17974
ISBN 0-87239-720-3

Phonetic Key to Pronunciation

a	as in sad
ai, ay	as in say
ah	as in top
	father
ee	as in me
e, eh	as in met
i, eye, y	as in idol
i, ih	as in tip
o, oh	as in over
au	as in power
yoo	as in unite
oo	as in rule
u, uh	as in alone
	item
	purify
	abandon
	hut
g	as in go
j	as in large
s, ss	as in list
	decide
k	as in car
kw	as in quick
f	as in alphabet
eks	as in extra
zh	as in decision
sh	as in action
th	as in thin
er	as in butter
	altar
	fur
	sir
	labor

Index to Maps and Charts

Abbreviations Used in This Book

n. — noun
v. — verb
adj. — adjective

OT — Old Testament
NT — New Testament

King Ahab (1 Kings 21)

Aa

Aaron (*air*-un): the older son of Amram and Jochebed, of the tribe of Levi. He was born during the captivity in Egypt. His younger brother was Moses and his sister was Miriam (Numbers 26:59). Aaron was appointed by God to be the spokesman for Moses during the exodus of the Israelites from Egypt and a helper as they wandered in the wilderness (Exodus 4:14-16; 7:19; 17:9-13). While Moses was on Mount Sinai, Aaron made a golden calf for the people to worship (Exodus 32:2-5). Later he was made the first high priest of the Israelite nation and served in that office the latter part of his life. He died at the age of 123, after his priestly robes and office were given to his son Eleazar (Numbers 20:28).

Abaddon (uh-*bad*-un): 1. ruin; destruction; 2. the place of the dead; the grave

abba (*ab*-buh): father

Abednego (uh-*bed*-nee-go): the Chaldean name given to Azariah, one of the friends of Daniel, when he was taken captive to Babylon. God saved him and his friends from death in the fiery furnace (Daniel 1:7; 3:12-30).

Abel: the second son of Adam and Eve. He was a shepherd and a righteous man. His brother Cain killed him in a rage of jealousy (Genesis 4:1-16). This was the first murder in the history of mankind.

Abiah (uh-*bye*-uh): see **Abijah**

abide: to endure; to last for a long time—**abiding**

Abihu (uh-*bye*-hyoo): son of Aaron and Elisheba (Exodus 6:23); a priest of the tabernacle (Exodus 28:1). He and his brother Nadab made an unacceptable offering to the Lord, and God killed them with fire (Leviticus 10:1, 2).

Abijah (uh-*bye*-juh): 1. the second son of Samuel. His father appointed him judge over Israel, but he became evil (1 Samuel 8:1-3; 1 Chronicles 6:28). He was also called Abiah; 2. son and successor of Rehoboam on the throne of Judah (1 Kings 14:31; 2 Chronicles 12:16—13:2). He ruled three years, beginning in about 959 B.C. He was also called Abijam; 3. a priest who entered into covenant with Nehemiah to walk in God's law (Nehemiah 10:7); 4. the mother of Hezekiah (2 Chronicles 29:1), also called Abi (2 Kings 18:2); 5. a chief of the priests who returned from Babylon with Zerubbabel (Nehemiah 12:4, 17)

Abimelech (uh-*bim*-uh-lek): 1. name of several Philistine kings; 2. one of the sons of Gideon. He killed 70 of his brothers and made himself king of Shechem. He died during an attack on Thebez (Judges 9).

Abinadab (uh-*bin*-uh-dab): 1. a Levite in whose house the ark of the covenant remained for about 20 years (1 Samuel 7:1, 2; 1 Chronicles 13:7); 2. second son of Jesse and brother of David. He followed Saul in his war against the Philistines (1 Samuel 16:8; 17:13); 3. a son of Saul who was killed with his brothers in a battle on Mount Gilboa (1 Samuel 31:2)

Abner: cousin of King Saul and leader of his army. He later joined David but was murdered by one of David's men (1 Samuel 14:50, 51; 2 Samuel 3:20-27).

abode: a home; a place to live

abolish (uh-*bahl*-ish): to do away with

abomination (uh-*bahm*-in-*ay*-shun): a disgusting and hateful thing

Abraham (*ay*-bruh-ham): the son of Terah, husband of Sarai (or Sarah), and uncle of Lot (Genesis 11:31). He was born in Ur of the Chaldees. When he was 75 years old he traveled with all his household to Canaan, as God had instructed him to do. Here God promised him that the land would be the inheritance of his descendants. He was called Abram until God changed his name to Abraham. God did this when He promised Abraham again that he would be the father of a great nation (Genesis 17:5). He had several sons, but the most favored was Isaac, the child promised by God when Abraham and Sarah were in their old age. Abraham died at the age of 175. He is known for his great faith. The record of his life can be found in Genesis 11:26—25:10.

Abram: see **Abraham**

Absalom (*ab*-suh-lum): the handsome son of King David. He plotted to gain his father's throne and almost succeeded. In a decisive battle at Gilead, Absalom's forces were defeated. While he was fleeing, his head was caught in the low branches of a tree, and he was murdered as he hung there (2 Samuel 13—18).

abstain: to deliberately do without

something, especially certain foods or drinks, for religious or health reasons—n. **abstinence** (*ab*-stih-nenss)

abundant (uh-*bun*-dunt): having more than enough; having plenty—n. **abundance**

accursed (uh-*kurst*): condemned to destruction and punishment

accuse (uh-*kyooz*): to blame; to charge someone with a fault or with wrongdoing—n. **accusation** (*ak*-kyoo-*zay*-shun)

Achaia (uh-*kay*-yuh): In the NT Achaia refers to the southern part of Greece. When the Romans conquered Greece, the emperor Augustus divided the country into two provinces, Macedonia and Achaia (Acts 19:21; Romans 15:26; 1 Thessalonians 1:7, 8). The province was governed by a proconsul or deputy (Acts 18:12), who was appointed by the Roman senate. The chief cities of Achaia were Athens and the capital, Corinth, where the proconsul lived. Its seaport was at Cenchrea, about seven miles east of the city on the Saronic Gulf.

Achan (*ay*-kun): an Israelite who took clothing, silver, and gold, part of the loot after the battle at Jericho. Because he disobeyed God in doing so, the Israelites lost a battle, and Achan and all his family were put to death (Joshua 7).

Achish (*ay*-kish): a Philistine king of Gath. David went to him for protection when he was fleeing from King Saul (1 Samuel 21:10-15).

acknowledge (ak-*nahl*-ij): 1. to admit knowing about something or agreeing with something; 2. to express gratitude or respect

Adam: the first man. God formed him from the dust of the ground and breathed into his nostrils, and man became a living soul (Genesis 2:7). Adam and his wife Eve disobeyed God and were driven from the Garden of Eden (Genesis 3).They had three sons whose names are given—Cain, Abel, and Seth—and other sons and daughters. Adam lived 930 years (Genesis 4:1—5:5).

Adam: a city on the east bank of the Jordan River. It was about a mile below the mouth of the Jabbok River and about 18 miles north of Jericho. Here the waters of the Jordan were held back for the miraculous crossing of the Israelites when they entered the promised land (Joshua 3:16).

adjure (uh-*joor*): 1. to plead or beg; 2. to ask someone under oath (in a courtroom, for example) to answer a question.

admonish (ad-*mahn*-ish): to warn against doing wrong; to reprove; to encourage

adoption (uh-*dahp*-shun): 1. taking a child into one's family and caring for him as if he were one's own child; 2. choosing or accepting something

Adramyttium (ad-rah-*mit*-tee-um): a seaport city of Mysia, in Asia. When Paul was sent from Caesarea to Rome, he was put on a ship of Adramyttium, about to sail to places on the coast of Asia (Acts 27:2).

Adullam (uh-*dul*-lum): a city in Judah between Jarmuth and Socoh (Joshua 15:35). Nearby was the cave of Adullam where David hid, and which he used as headquarters for his activities (1 Samuel 22; 2 Samuel 23:13).

adultery (uh-*dull*-ter-ee): having sexual relations with someone other than one's husband or wife

adversary (*ad*-ver-sair-ee): one that opposes; enemy; a name used in reference to Satan

Aeneas (eh-*nee*-us): a man in Lydda who had been sick with palsy for eight years. Peter healed him, and the church grew in that region (Acts 9:32-35).

Aenon (*ee*-nahn): John baptized here because there was much water (John 3:23). The exact location is not known, but some scholars locate Aenon west of the Jordan, eight miles south of Scythopolis or Bethshan.

affliction (uh-*flik*-shun): great trouble or suffering

Africa: the continent located south of the Mediterranean Sea, east of the Atlantic, and west of the Indian Ocean and Red Sea

Agabus (*ag*-uh-bus): a prophet living in Jerusalem in the time of the early church. He prophesied a worldwide famine (Acts 11:27-30) and warned Paul he would be arrested in Jerusalem (Acts 21:10, 11).

Agrippa (uh-*grip*-uh): see **Herod (3, 4)**

Ahab: the seventh king of Israel, son and successor of Omri. His wicked wife, Jezebel, influenced him to worship Baal and to allow idol worship in Israel. His pagan worship brought warnings from the prophet Elijah and resulted in the contest on Mount Carmel (1 Kings 18:17-40). Ahab died from an arrow wound received in battle (1 Kings 22:34-37).

Ahasuerus (ay-*haz*-yoo-ee-rus): a king of Persia; the same as Xerxes. After his queen, Vashti, had been dethroned, Esther was chosen to be his queen. Ahasuerus was friendly to the Jewish people (book of Esther).

Ahaz: twelfth king of Judah. He was weak; he worshiped idols, and offered his own son to a heathen god (2 Chronicles 28).

Ahaziah (ay-huh-*zye*-uh): a wicked king of Israel; son of Ahab and Jezebel. Worshiped the false god, Baal (2 Kings 1:1-17).

Ahijah (uh-*hye*-juh): 1. a Levite who was in charge of the treasures in the house of God in David's reign (1 Chronicles 26:20); 2. a prophet of Shiloh. He told Jeroboam that he would become king over ten of the tribes of Israel (1 Kings 11:29-39).

Ahikam (uh-*hye*-kum): son of Shaphan the scribe and a leader of Judah (2 Kings 22:12). He protected Jeremiah when priests and false prophets demanded Jeremiah's death (Jeremiah 26:24). After the Babylonian captivity, his son Gedaliah was made ruler over the few left in the cities (2 Kings 25:22).

Aholiab (uh-*ho*-lee-ab): son of Ahisamach, of the tribe of Dan. God gave him great skill in embroidery, weaving, and engraving, and through Moses appointed him and Bezaleel to lead in the construction of the tabernacle (Exodus 35:30-35).

Ai (*ay*-eye): a city of central Palestine, east of Bethel and about 12 miles north of Jerusalem. Abraham camped between Ai and Bethel on his return from Egypt (Genesis 12:8). Joshua conquered Ai after the Israelite victory at Jericho (Joshua 7, 8). It is sometimes called *Hai*.

alabaster (*al*-uh-bass-ter): a kind of soft stone, layered like marble, and used to make small boxes for ointment or perfume

Alexandria (al-eks-*an*-dree-uh): an important Greek city founded by Alexander the Great in 332 B.C. It is located in Egypt near the point where the western branch of the Nile River empties into the Mediterranean Sea. It was a great center of education as well as a commercial center, trading with Rome, India, Arabia, and parts of Africa. In NT times, it had a population of at least 600,000. About one-fourth of them were Jews, and the Jews had a large synagogue there. Some of them were among the persecutors of Stephen (Acts 6:9). Alexandria was the home of Apollos (Acts 18:24), and from its harbor sailed two of the grain ships used by the centurion to take Paul to Rome (Acts 27:6; 28:11).

Alexandrian (al-eks-*an*-dree-un): a native of the Egyptian city of Alexandria. Most of its inhabitants were Egyptians, Greeks, Romans, and Jews.

alleluia (al-lay-*loo*-ya): a Hebrew term of praise; "praise the Lord!"

almighty: all-powerful; a name given to God

alms (ahmz): charity; the giving of food, clothes, or money to the poor or the sick—**almsdeeds**

aloe (*al*-oh): perfume made from a tree that grew in lands far to the east of Israel; also used as a medicine

alpha (*al*-fuh): 1. first letter in the Greek alphabet; 2. the first; the beginning

Alpheus (al-*fee*-us): 1. the father of Matthew (Levi), the tax collector (Mark 2:14); 2. the father of James the apostle (Mark 3:18)

altar (*all*-ter): a mound of earth or stones on which to burn incense, or to make an animal sacrifice as an offering to God

altar

altar of burnt offering: a brass-covered platform, 7½ feet square and 4½ feet high, on which animals were sacrificed at the tabernacle. The altar stood east of the tabernacle near the entrance to the court. On two sides of the

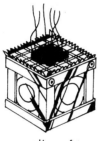

altar of burnt offering

altar were brass rings for poles to be run through so that the altar might be carried as the people moved through the wilderness.

altar of incense: a sacred stand, three feet high and 1½ feet square, covered with pure gold. It stood in the Holy Place in front of the veil separating it from the Most Holy Place. Incense was burned here morning and evening.

Alush (*ay*-lush): a place where the Israelites camped between Egypt and Mount Sinai (Numbers 33:13, 14)

Amalek (*am*-uh-lek): son of Eliphaz and grandson of Esau (Genesis 36:12;

1 Chronicles 1:36). His descendants were the Amalekites.

Amalekites: (am-uh-luh-kites): an ancient people who wandered about, dwelling mainly in a desert region to the south of Judea, from the time of Abraham to Hezekiah. They frequently raided the Israelites and are mentioned in Exodus 17, Numbers 14:45, and 1 Samuel 15.

Amaziah (am-uh-*zye*-uh): son of Joash; ninth king of Judah. One of the good kings (2 Kings 14:1-20)

ambassador (am-*bass*-uh-der): a messenger of high rank

amen (ah-men or ay-men): so be it; may it become true

amethyst (*am*-uh-thist): a precious stone, blue in color; a quartz rock

Amnon (*am*-non): oldest son of David; murdered by his half-brother, Absalom (2 Samuel 13)

Amon (*ay*-mun): fifteenth king of Judah, son of Manasseh; worshiped idols; killed by his servants after two years of wicked reign (2 Kings 21:18-25)

Amorites: people living in the hill country of Canaan when the Israelites conquered the land on their return from Egypt (Exodus 3:8; 33:2; Numbers 13:29). They were defeated by the Israelites, led by Joshua (Joshua 10:5-14).

Amos: a native of Tekoa in Judah, about six miles south of Bethlehem. He was a shepherd and a dresser of sycamore trees when God called him to be a prophet. He prophesied during the reigns of Uzziah, king of Judah, and Jeroboam II, king of Israel (Amos 1:1; 7:14, 15). His prophecies are recorded in the OT in the book of Amos. Its general theme is the judgment of God.

Amphipolis (am-*fip*-uh-lus): the capital city of one of the four districts into which Macedonia was divided. Paul passed through it as he journeyed from Philippi to Thessalonica (Acts 17:1).

Amram: a descendant of Levi, husband of Jochebed, and father of Aaron, Moses, and Miriam (Numbers 26:57-59)

amulet (*am*-yoo-let): a pendant or charm; an object that was worn or carried because it was thought the object was a magical protection against evil

amulet

Anak, Anakim (*ay*-nak, *an*-uh-kim): the name of a race of giants who founded the city of Hebron (Numbers 13:22). In the time of Moses, the Israelites were afraid of them (Numbers 13:28; Deuteronomy 9:2). They were driven from Canaan by Israel, led by Joshua (Joshua 11:21, 22), and Hebron was given to Caleb (Judges 1:20). The giant Goliath, of Gath, was probably one of the Anakim.

Ananias (an-uh-*nye*-us): 1. husband of Sapphira. They lied about their offering to the church, and were punished by death (Acts 5:1-11); 2. a disciple at Damascus who was sent by God to instruct Paul and cure him of his blindness (Acts 9:10-19); 3. a high priest before whom Paul was tried in Jerusalem (Acts 23:1-5).

Anathoth (*an*-uh-thahth): a city in the territory of Benjamin (Joshua 21:18). It was the birthplace of Jeremiah (Jeremiah 1:1).

Andrew: the brother of Simon Peter, of Bethsaida (John 1:44). He was a fisherman like Peter, and they shared a house in Capernaum (Mark 1:16-18, 21, 29-31). He was one of the 12 apostles (Mark 3:14-19). Andrew was the one who brought the lad with his lunch to Jesus to feed the 5,000 (John 6:1-14).

angel (*ain*-jel): a heavenly being used by God to send messages to man

Anna: daughter of Phanuel of the tribe of Asher. She became a prophetess, and at the age of 84 she recognized the baby Jesus as the Messiah when He was brought to the temple (Luke 2:36-38).

Annas: a high priest in Jerusalem from about A.D. 6-15. He was father-in-law of the high priest Caiaphas. Even though Annas was no longer officially in office when Jesus was arrested, he was still the most influential priest and still bore the title. Jesus was first examined by him and then sent to Caiaphas (Luke 3:2; John 18:13, 24). Months later Peter and John were brought before him (Acts 4:6).

anoint (uh-*noint*): to pour oil onto a person or thing, often as part of a ceremony to show that the person or thing has been chosen for a special purpose

anoint

anointed (uh-*noint*-ed): n. chosen by God for a special purpose; this name (Christ) was given to Jesus

Antioch (*an*-tee-ahk): 1. a town in Asia Minor, located in Pisidia near the border of Phrygia. After 25 B.C. Rome made it a part of the Roman province of Galatia. Jews lived in Antioch and had a synagogue (Acts 13:14). Paul and Barnabas visited it on their first missionary journey (Acts 13:14-52). Antioch was one of the churches to whom Paul wrote his letter to the Galatians; 2. the capital city of Syria. It was the third largest city in the Roman empire, with a population of about 500,000. It was located about 15 miles from the Mediterranean port of Seleucia. Great caravans from the north, east, and south came to its market-

places, while boats in the harbor brought their items of merchandise and waited to be refilled. Antioch played an important part in the history of the early church. Nicolas, one of the first seven deacons in the early church, was a proselyte from there (Acts 6:5). During the persecutions following the stoning of Stephen, many Christians from Jerusalem fled to Antioch and preached about Jesus. The first Gentile church was founded there. The Jerusalem church sent Barnabas to assist in the work, and he later called Paul to help him (Acts 11:19-26). The church at Antioch sent Paul and his companions out on his three missionary journeys (Acts 13:1ff; 15:35-41; 18:22, 23).

Apollonia (ap-puh-*lo*-nee-uh): a town in Macedonia. It was about 28 miles west of Amphipolis and 38 miles east of Thessalonica. The apostle Paul passed through Apollonia on his second missionary journey on his way from Philippi to Thessalonica (Acts 17:1).

Apollos (uh-*pahl*-us): a very educated Jew from Alexandria. Aquila and Priscilla helped him understand the Scriptures more fully (Acts 18:24-28). After this he became a preacher of the gospel (Acts 18:27; 1 Corinthians 3:4-6).

apostle (uh-*pahs*-sul): one who is sent forth on a special mission

Appii Forum (*ap*-ee-eye *fo*-rum): a town on the Appian Way in Italy, about 40

miles southeast of Rome. Christians from Rome met Paul there (Acts 28:15).

appoint (uh-*point*): to arrange; to fix or set officially, as in setting a date or naming someone to a position

Aquila (*ak*-wih-luh): a Jew from Pontus; husband of Priscilla. They were refugees from Rome and had a tentmaking business in Corinth. Because Paul followed the same trade, he lived and worked with them. They also instructed Apollos more fully in the Scriptures (Acts 18). The church in Ephesus met in their home (1 Corinthians 16:19).

Arabia (uh-*ray*-bee-uh): a peninsula comprising a desert area in southwest Asia. It was bound on the west by the Red Sea, on the south by the Indian Ocean, on the east by the Persian Gulf, and on the north by modern Jordan, Syria, and Iraq. Originally it was the northern part of the peninsula between the Red Sea and the Persian Gulf (Isaiah 21:13; Ezekiel 27:21), but later the entire peninsula (Nehemiah 2:19; Galatians 1:17). People from Arabia were present in Jerusalem on the Day of Pentecost (Acts 2:11).

Arabians (uh-*ray*-bee-unz): those of the Arab race. They were the wandering tribes living in the country to the east and south of Palestine. In the early times of Hebrew history, they were known as Ishmaelites and descendants of Keturah, Abraham's second wife (Genesis 25:1-4, 13-18).

Athens (Acts 17)

Aramaic (air-uh-*may*-ik): the language spoken by the Jews at the time of Christ, especially in Galilee

Ararat (*air*-uh-rat): a high plateau on the far eastern border of modern Turkey, north of Biblical Haran and about midway between the Black and Caspian Seas, near the junction of Turkey, Armenia, and Iran (Persia). The Tigris and Euphrates Rivers are formed from streams flowing from this mountainous area. Noah's ark rested on one of the mountains of Ararat (Genesis 8:4).

Archelaus (ahr-kih-*lay*-us): son of Herod the Great and ruler of Judea when Mary, Joseph, and Jesus returned from Egypt. Joseph was afraid of this cruel ruler and bypassed the area on his way to Nazareth (Matthew 2:22).

Archippus (ahr-*kip*-us): a Christian and officer in the church in Colosse (Colossians 4:17). He was a fellow worker with Philemon (Philemon 2).

Areopagus (air-ee-*ahp*-uh-gus): 1. a rocky point on the west side of the Acropolis at Athens, called Mars' Hill in Acts 17; 2. the name of the council that met on Mars' Hill. Paul spoke before this group (Acts 17:22-34).

Aristarchus (air-is-*tahr*-kus): a Christian from Thessalonica and travel companion of Paul (Acts 19:29; 20:4; 27:2; Colossians 4:10; Philemon 24).

ark: 1. a large boat made of gopher wood and covered with pitch. It was built by Noah according to God's instructions, and used to save Noah's family and some animals when God sent a flood to destroy the earth; 2. a basket covered with pitch made by the mother of Moses.

ark of the covenant (*kuv*-uh-nent): a chest, 3¾ feet long and 2½ feet wide and high, covered with pure gold, having two cherubim on the lid. The ark was kept in the Most Holy Place of the tabernacle and later in the temple. It contained the law written on tablets of stone, a pot of manna, and Aaron's rod.

ark of the covenant

armor, armour: metal covering worn to

protect the body of a soldier during battle.

Arnon (*ahr*-non): river that empties into the Dead Sea a little north of center, at about the lowest point on the surface of the earth. In the time of Moses the Arnon was the boundary between the Moabites and the Amorites (Numbers 21:13). For many years it was the southern boundary for the tribe of Reuben.

array (uh-*ray*): v. 1. to set something in order; 2. to decorate or dress up something

array: n. 1. an arrangement; 2. clothing

art: are

Artaxerxes (ahr-tuh-zerk-zeez): a Persian king who, in about 458 B.C., permitted Nehemiah to lead a great number of the Jews back to Jerusalem to rebuild the walls of the city (Nehemiah 2:1-8).

ascension (uh-*sen*-shun): 1. the act of rising or going up; 2. the name given to Jesus' return to Heaven after His resurrection.

Ashdod: one of the five leading Philistine cities, located nine miles northeast of Askelon, three miles east of the Mediterranean Sea, and 18 miles north of Gaza. Anakim remained here after the conquest of Canaan by the Hebrews (Joshua 11:22). The ark of God was carried to Ashdod after the

Philistines captured it at Ebenezer (1 Samuel 5:1-8). In NT times the city was called Azotus. Philip preached in the area between this place and Caesarea (Acts 8:40).

Asher: the eighth son of Jacob. Zilpah was his mother (Genesis 30:12, 13). He was the founder of one of the 12 tribes of Israel.

Asia: the great continent east of Europe and Africa. Asia Minor was the western area of Asia by the Black, Aegean, and Mediterranan Seas. In NT times, the Roman province that contained the southwest part of Asia Minor included the countries of Mysia, Lydia, Caria, most of Phrygia, plus several islands and coastal cities. Its capital was Ephesus. Jews from Asia were present in Jerusalem on the Day of Pentecost (Acts 2:9). Paul visited this area on his missionary travels (Acts 19:10).

assay (*ass*-say): 1. to try or attempt to do something; 2. to judge the worth of something

assurance (uh-*shoor*-unss): 1. certainty; confidence; being sure; 2. being safe and secure

Assyria (uh-*seer*-ee-uh): a country east of the Tigris River, bounded on the north by the mountains of Armenia, on the east by the Median ranges, and on the south by the environs of Nineveh, later its capital city. In about 722 B.C. the Assyrians captured Samaria and took the Israelites into captivity (2 Kings 15:29; 17:6). In 612 B.C. Nineveh was destroyed by the Babylonians and the Medes, and the Assyrian power came to an end.

astrologer (uh-*strahl*-uh-jer): a person who studied the stars because he believed that the future could be determined from knowing their movements

Athaliah (ath-uh-*lye*-uh): daughter of Ahab and Jezebel. When her son Ahaziah was killed, she seized the throne and had all his sons killed except one, Joash. Joash was stolen by his aunt and hidden for six years. When Joash was crowned king, Athaliah was taken out and killed (2 Kings 11:1-16).

Athens: the capital city of the state of Attica in Greece. Today it is the capital of Greece. In ancient times it had a population of almost a quarter of a million. It was the center of world culture, making contributions in the areas of government, architecture, literature, art, and philosophy. It was wholly given to idolatry and had many beautiful temples built to the gods and goddesses. In NT times, Athens was subject to Rome. On his second missionary journey, Paul preached on Mars' Hill in Athens (Acts 17).

atonement (uh-*tone*-ment): 1. reconciliation; becoming friends again with someone who had been an enemy; 2. being forgiven for our sins through a sacrifice acceptable to God. This was done through the shedding of blood—in the OT, animals were sacrificed, and in the NT, Jesus was the complete and final sacrifice to take away the sins of mankind.

Attalia (at-*tal*-lee-uh): a Mediterranean seaport on the coast of Pamphylia, near Perga, in southern Asia Minor. Paul visited there on his first missionary journey (Acts 14:25).

authority (uh-*thor*-ih-tee): 1. the power or right to command people; 2. the people or government with the power or right to command other people

avenge (uh-*venj*): to gain satisfaction by punishing someone for a wrong he has done—*n.* **avenger**

Azariah (az-uh-rye-uh): a common name among Hebrew families. Some of the principal people in the OT with this name were 1. a king of Judah (see Uzziah); 2. the high priest during the reign of King Solomon (1 Kings 4:2-5); 3. a prophet, son of Obed, who encouraged King Asa so that a great religious reform took place (2 Chronicles 15:1-8); 4. high priest in the reign of King Uzziah of Judah. He protested when the king tried to assume priestly functions (2 Chronicles 26:16-20); 5. the original and Hebrew name of Abednego (Daniel 1:6, 7)

Azotus (uh-*zo*-tus): see **Ashdod**

Balaam (Numbers 22)

Bb

Baal (*bay*-ul): a false god worshiped by many of the heathen peoples of Canaan, often with self-torture and human sacrifice; the word meant "master" or "lord"

Babel, tower of (*bay*-bul): a huge tower that the people of Shinar attempted to build shortly after the flood. God stopped them by confusing their languages (Genesis 11:1-9).

Babylon (*bab*-uh-lahn): 1. the capital city of Babylonia. Babylon was an important city in southern Mesopotamia, and was famous for its hanging gardens, temples, and palaces; 2. the country of Babylonia

Babylonia (bab-uh-*lo*-nee-uh): an area of the lower Euphrates and Tigris Rivers in western Asia. It was bounded on the north by Assyria, on the east by the mountains of Elam, on the south by the Persian Gulf, and on the west by the Arabian desert. The country is sometimes called Shinar (Genesis 10:10, 11) or "land of the Chaldeans" (Jeremiah 24:5; 25:12). Under Babylonia's best-known king, Nebuchadnezzar, the kingdom of Judah was taken into captivity (2 Kings 24, 25).

Balaam (*bay*-lum): a prophet whom Balak, king of Moab, hired to curse Israel so that Balak could drive them away. On his way to the king, Balaam had a frightening experience with an angel and a talking donkey. Then, instead of cursing Israel, Balaam prophesied great blessings from God for them (Numbers 22—24).

balm: a gum or thick juice obtained from the balsam tree. The pale yellow, sweet-smelling gum was used for incense, and when dissolved in water it was used as an ointment for wounds. The oil, made from the bark, leaves, and berries, was used as a medicine.

baptism (*bap*-tiz-um): *n.* 1. being immersed or put under water; 2. part of the Great Commission (Matthew 28:19; Mark 16:15); 3. a symbol of the death, burial and resurrection of Jesus (Romans 6); 4. being initiated into something—*v.* **baptize**

Barabbas (buh-*rab*-us): a thief and a murderer in prison when Jesus was arrested. The Jews chose to free him instead of Jesus, whom they crucified (Matthew 27:15-26).

Barak (*bair*-ak): the son of Abinoam, from Kedesh-Naphtali. He was commanded by Deborah, judge of Israel, to lead the Israelite army against Jabin, king of Hazor (Judges 4).

barbarous (*bar*-buh-rus): cruel or harsh; savage or uncivilized

bare: gave birth to

Bar-Jesus: see **Elymas**

barley (*bar*-lee): a grain grown for food, used both by people and animals

Barnabas (*bar*-nuh-bus): the surname of Joses (Joseph), a Levite from Cyprus who was converted to Christianity. He sold his land and gave the price of it to the apostles (Acts 4:36, 37). When the Christians in Jerusalem were afraid to receive Paul, Barnabas spoke on his behalf (Acts 9:27). He worked with Paul in Antioch (Acts 11:22-26) and on Paul's first missionary journey (Acts 13, 14). Paul spoke highly of Barnabas (1 Corinthians 9:6; Galatians 2:1, 9, 13; and Colossians 4:10).

barren (*bair*-en): 1. unable to produce life; desolate; empty; 2. without child

Bartholomew (bar-*thahl*-uh-myoo): one of the 12 apostles (Matthew 10:3; Mark 3:18; Luke 6:14; Acts 1:13). Bartholomew is probably the surname of Nathanael, who was led to Christ by Philip (John 1:45, 46).

Bartimeus (bar-tih-*mee*-us): a blind beggar in Jericho who received his sight by the healing power of Jesus (Mark 10:46-52)

Baruch (*bair*-uk): a friend and scribe of Jeremiah. Baruch wrote the prophecies of Jeremiah as he dictated them (Jeremiah 36:4).

basin, bason (*bay*-sun): a large bowl or container

Bathsheba (bath-*shee*-buh): the beautiful wife of Uriah to whom David was attracted. David arranged to have Uriah killed in battle, so he could marry her (2 Samuel 11, 12). She was the mother of four sons: Solomon, Shimea, Shobab, and Nathan (1 Chronicles 3:5). *Bathshua* is another spelling for Bathsheba.

beatitudes (bee-*at*-uh-tyoodz): a name given to the statements made by Jesus that begin with the words "blessed are" (Matthew 5:3-12) in His sermon on the mount

beckon: to summon someone by nodding the head or waving the hand

bed: in Jesus' time, usually a heavy roll or mat that was placed upon the floor at night to sleep on and taken up during the day

Beersheba: a city in southern Palestine, about midway between the southern end of the Dead Sea and the Mediterranean. It was the most southern city in the land (Judges 20:1; 1 Samuel 3:20). In this area Hagar wandered with her son Ishmael (Genesis 21:14-18). Abraham lived here after he offered Isaac on Mount Moriah (Genesis 22:19). Here God spoke to Isaac (Genesis 26:23, 24). God appeared at this place to Jacob as he journeyed to Egypt (Genesis 46:1-7). Elijah sought refuge from the wicked Jezebel in Beersheba (1 Kings 19:3). The modern city of Beersheba (or Beer-sheva) is an important center for Israeli settlements.

befall: to happen

beget (bee-get): 1. to father a child; 2. to cause—*past tense,* **begat**

begotten (bee-got-ten): born to a father

beguile (bee-gile): 1. to persuade by being tricky or cunning; 2. to cheat, mislead, or deceive

behold (bee-hold): an exclamation meaning "Look!"

believe (bee-leev): 1. to accept trustfully and on faith; 2. to consider something to be true and real

Belshazzar (bel-shaz-er): a famous king of Babylon. He used the sacred vessels from the temple in Jerusalem at a drunken feast. Miraculous handwriting appeared on the wall, and Daniel interpreted it to mean the overthrow of the kingdom (Daniel 5). That night Belshazzar was killed and his kingdom destroyed by the Persian army.

Belteshazzar (bel-tuh-shaz-zer): See **Daniel**

Ben-Hadad (ben—hay-dad): title for kings of Syria. This nation and Israel were continually at war until both were overcome by Assyria. They are mentioned in 1 Kings 15, 20; 2 Kings 6—8, 13.

Benjamin: the second and youngest son of Jacob by Rachel (Genesis 35:24), and Joseph's full brother. The tribe of Benjamin was named for him. King Saul, Jeremiah, and Saul of Tarsus were from his tribe.

Berea (buh-ree-uh): a city in southern Macedonia. It was about 50 miles southwest of Thessalonica, the chief city of Macedonia at that time. Paul and Silas spent some time in Berea and started a church there. Paul commended the Christians there for their careful study of the Scriptures (Acts 17:10-14; 20:4). Sometimes spelled *Beroea.*

Berean (buh-*ree*-un): a native of Berea. The Christians in Berea are remembered for their thorough study of the Scriptures.

Bernice (ber-*nye*-see): daughter of Herod Agrippa I (Acts 12:1). She was with her brother Agrippa II when Paul made his defense before him in Caesarea (Acts 25:13—26:32).

beryl (bur-el): a type of precious stone, usually yellow in color

beseech: to ask, plead, or beg for something

Bethabara (beth-*ab*-uh-ruh): a place east of the Jordan River where John was baptizing (John 1:28). This might be the site of the present day Abarah, about 12 miles south of the Sea of Galilee and northeast of Beth-shean.

Bethany: 1. a village on the east side of the Mount of Olives, about two miles from Jerusalem. Jesus often stayed there (Matthew 21:17; 26:6; Mark 11:1, 11, 12; 14:3). It was the home of Mary, Martha, and Lazarus (John 11:1; 12:1), as well as Simon the leper (Matthew 26:6-13; Mark 14:3). Jesus ascended to Heaven near there (Luke 24:50, 51); 2. "Bethany beyond the Jordan," where John baptized (John 1:28); possibly the same as Bethabara.

Bethel: a town about 12 miles north of Jerusalem, originally called Luz (Genesis 28:19; Joshua 18:13). Here Abram camped (Genesis 12:8; 13:3). Jacob had a dream here on his way to Padanaram (Genesis 28:19). Samuel judged here (1 Samuel 7:16). Jeroboam made Bethel one of the two places of worship for Israel, and erected a golden calf there (1 Kings 12:28-33).

Books of the Bible

Old Testament	2 Chronicles	Hosea	**New Testament**	Colossians
	Ezra	Joel		1 Thessalonians
Law	Nehemiah	Amos	**Gospels**	2 Thessalonians
Genesis	Esther	Obadiah	Matthew	1 Timothy
Exodus		Jonah	Mark	2 Timothy
Leviticus	**Poetry**	Micah	Luke	Titus
Numbers	Job	Nahum	John	Philemon
Deuteronomy	Psalms	Habakkuk		Hebrews
	Proverbs	Zephaniah	**History**	James
History	Ecclesiastes	Haggai	Acts	1 Peter
Joshua	Song of Solomon	Zechariah		2 Peter
Judges		Malachi	**Letters**	1 John
Ruth	**Prophecy**		Romans	2 John
1 Samuel	Isaiah		1 Corinthians	3 John
2 Samuel	Jeremiah		2 Corinthians	Jude
1 Kings	Lamentations		Galatians	
2 Kings	Ezekiel		Ephesians	**Prophecy**
1 Chronicles	Daniel		Philippians	Revelation

Bethlehem (Matthew 2)

Bethlehem: a village on a Judean hill about five miles south of Jerusalem on the road to Hebron. Rachel was buried near Bethlehem (Genesis 35:16-19). It was the home of Izban (Judges 12:8-10), Elimelech (Ruth 1:1, 2), and Boaz (Ruth 2:1-4). As the birthplace and home of David, it was the "city of David" (Luke 2:4, 11). David was anointed to be king by Samuel at Bethlehem (1 Samuel 16:1-13). Jesus was born here (Matthew 2:1; Luke 2:1-18).

Bethphage (*beth*-fuh-jee): a village on the eastern slope of the Mount of Olives near or on the road from Jerusalem to Jericho. It is mentioned in connection with Jesus' journey from Bethany to Jerusalem on the day of the triumphal entry (Matthew 21:1; Mark 11:1 Luke 19:29).

Bethsaida (beth-*say*-ih-duh): a town located east of the place where the Jordan River flows into the Sea of Galilee. It was the home of Andrew, Peter, and Philip (John 1:44; 12:21). It was the scene of the feeding of the 5,000 (Luke 9:10). Jesus restored sight to a blind man in Bethsaida (Mark 8:22).

Beth-shan, Beth-shean: the most important fortress guarding any of the Jordan crossings, located about 14 miles south of the Sea of Galilee at the junction of the Plain of Jezreel with the Jordan Valley. Joshua was unable to capture Beth-shan (Joshua 17:16). After Saul died at Gilboa, the Philistines fastened his body to the wall of Beth-shan (1 Samuel 31:8-12). Later the city was also known as Scythopolis.

Beth-shemish (beth—*shee*-mish): a town of northwest Judah near the Philistine border. The ark of the covenant was brought here by the Philistines. Many people died because they dared to look inside the sacred ark (1 Samuel 6:7-21).

Bethuel (beth-*yoo*-ul): son of Nahor and Milcah, nephew of Abraham, and father of Rebekah and Laban (Genesis 24:15, 29)

Bezaleel (bee-*zal*-ee-el): son of Uri, grandson of Hur, of the tribe of Judah, and an expert at cutting stones, carving timber, and working with gold, silver, and brass. He helped in building the tabernacle and taught others to work (Exodus 35:30-35).

Bible: the name, meaning "book," that we give to the Word of God (see the Books of the Bible chart on p. 19).

Bilhah (*bil*-huh): a handmaid of Rachel (Genesis 29:29), and mother of Jacob's sons Dan and Naphtali (Genesis 35:25)

bind: 1. to tie up; 2. to restrain; 3. to bandage a wound; 4. to hold someone to obey the law or an agreement

birthright: special rights or privileges that went to the oldest son in a family, including twice as much property as any other son inherited and the right to become head of the family after his father's death.

bishop: elder; pastor; a spiritual leader of the church who is able to teach and help other church members

Bithynia (bih-*thin*-ee-uh): a Roman province in northwestern Asia Minor. Paul and his companions desired to go to Bithynia, but the Holy Spirit restrained them (Acts 16:6-10). However, there were Christians in Bithynia (1 Peter 1:1).

blame: *v.* to accuse or find fault with

blame: *n.* 1. responsibility; 2. fault; sin

blaspheme (blass-feem): *v.* to speak about God or about sacred things with abuse or contempt; to make fun of or insult God, Jesus, or the Holy Spirit; for any man but Jesus to claim to be God

blasphemy (*blass*-fuh-mee): *n.* anything that is spoken that is false about or insulting to God, Jesus, or the Holy Spirit; for someone other than God to claim to be God—*adj.* **blasphemous**

blemish: an imperfection, flaw, or defect that spoils something's appearance

bless: 1. to make holy or sacred; 2. to make happy or successful; 3. to ask God's kindness or favor for someone; 4. to praise—*n.* **blessing**

blessed (*bless*-ed): *adj.* 1. held in honor; 2. enjoying happiness

Boaz (*bo*-az): a wealthy man of Bethlehem, and a relative of Elimelech, the husband of Naomi. He married Ruth the Moabitess. He was the ancestor of David and Christ (book of Ruth; Matthew 1:5).

boisterous (*boy*-ster-us): noisy and excited; rowdy; high-spirited

bondage (*bahn*-dij): 1. being held captive as a slave; being under the control of someone else; 2. being a slave to sin

bondman: a slave—**bondwoman**

book: in Bible times what was called a book was actually a scroll

booth: a small shelter made of branches and vines, used during the Feast of Tabernacles

booth

booty: plunder; goods taken during a robbery or from an enemy during a war

bowels: 1. the insides of a person or animal; 2. the center of the emotions (as we now use the word "heart")

brake: broke

brazen: made of brass

brazen sea

brazen sea: a huge laver (basin) that stood in front of Solomon's temple. The laver was 15 feet in diameter and eight feet deep, set on twelve brazen oxen, and held water for the priests to wash in as part of the religious ceremony.

breach (breech): *n.* 1. the breaking of a law; 2. a break or gap in something, like a wall

breach: *v.* to break or violate

bread: often used in the Bible to mean food in general

breaking of bread: 1. eating a meal; 2. having the Lord's Supper together

breastplate: part of a soldier's armor; a heavy metal plate worn over the chest for protection

brethren: 1. brothers; 2. other Christians

bridle: leather straps fastened to a horse's head, used for guiding the horse

brimstone: sulfur, a substance that catches fire and burns very easily

buckler: a small round shield worn on the arm for protection in battle

bullock (*bull*-uk): a young bull. Bullocks were offered as sacrifices in worship to God during OT times; they were also used as work animals.

bulrushes: tall slender plants that grow in wet places. They were used to make papyrus, an ancient writing material. The mother of Moses used bulrushes to weave the basket-ark for her baby.

burnt offering: a male lamb, ram, goat, or young bull that was used to offer a sacrifice to God. The blood of the animal was sprinkled, smeared, or poured on the altar and then the entire animal was burned on the altar. This was an act of worship in OT times. After the death of Jesus, no more sacrifices were needed.

a chariot of fire (2 Kings 2)

Cc

Caesar (see-zer): Caesar was the title taken by each of the Roman emperors. Caesar Augustus ruled when Jesus was born (Luke 2:1); his successor, Tiberius Caesar, reigned A.D. 14-37 (Luke 3:1); Claudius Caesar reigned A.D. 41-54 (Acts 11:28; 18:2); and Nero reigned A.D. 54-68 (Acts 25:10-12; Philippians 4:22).

Caesarea (sess-er-ee-uh): a city on the coast of the Mediterranean Sea about 23 miles south of Mount Carmel, 30 miles north of Joppa, and 65 miles northwest of Jerusalem. It was built by Herod the Great in 22 B.C. Philip the evangelist (one of the first seven deacons, Acts 6:5), lived in Caesarea (Acts 21:8-10). It was the home of Cornelius, in whose house Peter first preached to the Gentiles (Acts 10). Paul was held prisoner in Caesarea for two years (Acts 23:23—26:32).

Caesarea Philippi (fih-lip-eye): a city north of the Sea of Galilee on the southwest slope of Mount Hermon at the main source of the Jordan River. This city was the scene of Peter's confession that Jesus is "the Christ, the Son of the living God" (Matthew 16:13-17).

Caiaphas (kay-uh-fuss): high priest in Jerusalem at the time of Jesus, about A.D. 17-36. He was the son-in-law of Annas. He proposed the death of Jesus (John 11:47-53). When Jesus was arrested, He was taken first to Annas, who sent Him to Caiaphas (John 18:13, 24). Caiaphas also took part in the trial of Peter and John (Acts 4:6).

Cain: the first son of Adam and Eve. He was a farmer. He killed his brother Abel in a jealous rage, and God punished him (Genesis 4; Hebrews 11:4).

Caleb (kay-lub): son of Jephunneh, of the tribe of Judah, one of the 12 men

Moses sent to spy out the land of Canaan. Caleb and Joshua were the only ones of the 12 spies who told the people to go and take the land (Numbers 13, 14).

Calvary (*kal*-vuh-ree): a Latin word meaning "the place of the skull;" the place outside Jerusalem where Jesus was crucified

Cana (*kay*-nuh): a village in Galilee a few miles north of Nazareth. Here Jesus performed His first miracle (John 2:1-11) and healed the nobleman's son who was in Capernaum (John 4:46). It was Nathanael's home (John 21:2).

Canaan (*kay*-nun): Canaan refers to Palestine west of the Jordan (Genesis 13:12). It was the land promised to Abraham and his descendants (Genesis 17:8). According to Genesis 10:15-20, Canaan extended from Sidon to Gaza, west of the Jordan.

Canaan (*kay*-nun): fourth son of Ham; grandson of Noah. All of the Canaanite tribes were descended from him (Genesis 10:6, 15-20).

Canaanites (*kay*-nun-ites): 1. the tribe that lived in a particular area of the land west of the Jordan River before the conquest of the Israelites; 2. the people who lived generally in the whole area of Canaan. The Canaanites were doomed to destruction because of their wickedness (Deuteronomy 20:17), but the Israelites were never able to overcome them completely.

Candace (*kan*-duh-see): a queen from Ethiopia (Acts 8:27). The name was not the name of an individual, but a title for a dynasty of Ethiopian queens (like "Pharaoh" for Egyptian kings and "Caesar" for Roman emperors).

candle: a small lamp with a wick, in which oil was burned

candlestick, golden: this was a large stand holding seven lamps filled with olive oil. It was made of pure gold, shaped like a tree trunk with six branches, and it stood on the south side of the tabernacle.

golden candlestick

canker: 1. an infected sore; 2. a kind of caterpillar

canst: can

Capernaum (kuh-*per*-nee-um): a city on the northwest shore of the Sea of Galilee where Jesus made His headquarters during His ministry in Galilee (Matthew 4:13; Mark 2:1). Jesus performed many miracles there, among them the healing of the centurion's servant (Matthew 8:5-13), the man lowered through the roof by his friends (Mark 2:1-12), and Peter's mother-in-law (Luke 4:38, 39). Jesus called Matthew, the tax collector, to be His apostle in Capernaum (Matthew 9:9-13). Even though Jesus worked and taught in the city, the people did

a carpenter's shop

not repent, and Jesus predicted the complete ruin of the city (Matthew 11:23, 24; Luke 10:15).

Cappadocia (kap-uh-*do*-see-uh): a Roman province in the eastern part of Asia Minor. It was a wild, barren, mountainous country. People from Cappadocia were in Jerusalem on the Day of Pentecost (Acts 2:9). Peter addresses one of his epistles to scattered Christians in this province (1 Peter 1:1).

captivity (kap-*tiv*-uh-tee): being held by force as a prisoner, especially in a foreign land

caravan (*kair*-uh-van): a group of travelers making a journey together

Carchemish (*kar*-kuh-mish): an ancient city of the Hittites located on the upper Euphrates River about 63 miles northeast of Aleppo. It was about 60 miles west of Haran. Pharaoh-necho of Egypt was defeated there by Nebuchadnezzar of Babylon (Jeremiah 46:2).

Carmel: a mountain range jutting into the Mediterranean Sea just south of the modern city of Haifa and west of the Sea of Galilee. In a contest on Mount Carmel the prophet Elijah defeated the prophets of Baal (1 Kings 18). The prophet Elisha visited Carmel (2 Kings 2:25; 4:25).

carnal (*kar*-nul): concerned with physical matters rather than spiritual ones; concerned with physical pleasures such as eating, comfort, or sexual pleasure

carpenter: a person who worked with wood, and perhaps also with stone and metal. Carpenters mainly made doors, window shutters, and farm implements like plows and yokes.

Casiphia (kuh-*sif*-ee-uh): a place in northern Babylonia near the route between Babylon and Jerusalem. The Levites in exile lived here (Ezra 8:17).

cease (seess): to stop; to bring to an end

cedar (*see*-dur): a large evergreen tree

Cedron (*see*-drun): See **Kidron**

Cenchrea, Cenchreae (sen-kree-uh): a seaport of Corinth on the Saronic Gulf about seven miles from the city. Paul embarked from Cenchrea after his first visit to Corinth (Acts 18:18). Phoebe was a servant in the church there (Romans 16:1).

censer (*sen*-sur): a holder for burning incense

centurion (sen-*tyoor*-ee-un): a Roman captain who had command of one hundred men

ceremony (*sair*-uh-mo-nee): a service or act that is planned, formal, and done according to prescribed procedures

chaff: 1. the covering of the seed that is separated during threshing; 2. something that is worthless

chalcedony (kal-*sed*-uh-nee): a pale blue precious stone

Chaldea (kal-*dee*-uh): originally it was the southern part of Babylonia, but later the term referred to the entire country. Babylonia is sometimes referred to as "the land of the Chaldeans" (Jeremiah 24:5; 25:12). This country conquered Judah and carried its people into captivity in about 586 B.C. (2 Kings 25:1-26; 2 Chronicles 36:11-21).

Chaldean (kal-*dee*-un): a person from Chaldea, the country of which Babylon was the capital

chamber: a room in a house

chamberlain (*chaim*-ber-lin): a chief officer in a king's household; an attendant for a king

chariot (*chair*-ee-ut): a cart with two wheels pulled by horses, used for war and for traveling long distances

charity: love; goodwill

chasten (*chay*-sun): to discipline; to purify; to punish, so that the one punished might become better

chastise (chass-*tize*): to punish

Chebar (*kee*-bar): a river in Babylonia. Some Jewish exiles, including the prophet Ezekiel, settled on the banks of this river. It was there Ezekiel saw some of his visions (Ezekiel 1:1, 3; 3:23; 10:15, 20).

Cherith (*kee*-rith): a brook flowing into the Jordan River, probably from the east, where God told Elijah to hide from Ahab. Here Elijah was miraculously fed by ravens (1 Kings 17:1-6).

cherub (*chair*-ub): a heavenly being, often used to guard something sacred—*pl.*, **cherubim**

Chilion (*kil*-ee-on): Son of Naomi and Elimelech; husband of Orpah (Ruth 1:2-5; 4:9, 10)

Chinnereth, Chinneroth (*kin*-uh-reth, -rahth): 1. an early name for the Sea of Galilee (Numbers 34:11; Deuteronomy 3:17; Joshua 11:2); 2. a fortified city of Naphtali (Joshua 19:35); 3. a district of Naphtali that was west of the Sea of Galilee. It was an area around the city of Chinnereth, usually identified with the plain of Genessaret (Matthew 14:34).

Chios (*kye*-ahs): a mountainous island at the entrance of the Aegean Sea about five miles from the mainland of Asia Minor. Paul's ship passed it as he returned to Jerusalem (Acts 20:15).

Chittim (*kit*-um): See **Cyprus**

Chorazin (kuh-*ray*-zin): a town northwest of the Sea of Galilee, about two miles north of Capernaum. Jesus ministered there, but the people rejected His message (Matthew 11:20-22; Luke 10:13).

Christ: "the anointed;" a Greek word for the Hebrew word *Messiah;* a title given Jesus

Christian: one who believes and obeys Jesus Christ; this name was first given to His followers at Antioch

chrysolite (*kris*-uh-lite): a transparent precious stone, the color of gold mixed with green

chrysoprasus (krih-*sop*-ruh-sus): a precious stone that is pale green in color

church: Christians; the assembly; those who belong to Christ

Cilicia (sih-*lish*-ee-uh): a district in southeast Asia Minor. Tarsus, its chief city, was the birthplace of the apostle Paul (Acts 21:39). Jews from Cilicia disputed with Stephen (Acts 6:9). The gospel reached Cilicia very early (Acts 15:23), probably through Paul (Acts 9:30; Galatians 1:21).

circumcision (*ser*-kum-*sizh*-un): the cutting off of the foreskin of a male; a religious rite given by God as a sign of the special relationship between Him and Abraham and all Abraham's descendants

clamor, clamour (*klam*-er): to cry, shout; make noise

Clauda: a small island about 23 miles off the southwestern coast of Crete. While on his way to Rome, a storm drove the ship carrying Paul to the island (Acts 27:16).

Cleopas: (*klee*-oh-pus): one of the two disciples who journeyed to and from Emmaus on the evening of the day Jesus arose from the dead (Luke 24:13-35)

cleave (kleev): 1. to stick close to someone or something; 2. to divide or split

cloak (kloke): a long, loose coat

closet: a private room; a secret place

clout: *v.* to strike or hit

clout: *n.* a piece of garment; rag

Cnidus (*nye*-dus): a city of Caria on the southwestern coast of Asia Minor. Paul sailed past Cnidus on his way to Rome (Acts 27:7).

cock: a rooster

Colossae, Colosse (kuh-*lahs*-see): a city on the Lycus River in Phrygia in southwestern Asia Minor. It was located about 12 miles from Laodicea. Colossae was on the most important trade route from Ephesus to Tarsus and Syria. The church in Colossae was probably started by Epaphras (Colossians 1:7, 8). Paul had not visited the church there before he wrote his epistle (Colossians 2:1).

comely (*kum*-lee): beautiful—*n.* **comeliness**

commandment: a law or ordinance

commit (kum-*mit*): 1. to trust somebody else to use or care for something of yours; 2. to promise to do something; 3. to put into action deliberately (for example, to *commit* a crime)

commitment (kuh-*mit*-ment): a promise to do something

commodious (kum-*mo*-dee-us): 1. roomy, spacious; 2. handy or available

compass (*kum*-pass): to travel entirely around something; encircle

compassion (kum-*pash*-un): sympathy; the desire to help others when they are in trouble; pity

commune (kum-*myoon*): to talk over or discuss

Communion: see **Lord's Supper**

conceive (kun-*seev*): 1. to become pregnant; 2. to cause something to begin; 3. to think of something

conception (kun-*sep*-shun): 1. the act of becoming pregnant; 2. the beginning of an idea

concubine (*kahn*-kyoo-bine): in times when a man was allowed to be married to more than one woman, a concubine was married to a man but did not have the importance or the privileges of a wife

coney

condemn (kun-*dem*): to pronounce guilty; to convict—*n.* **condemnation**

coney: a rabbit-like animal with short legs and ears and no tail

confession (kun-*feh*-shun): something that is told or made known, like 1. an admission of one's sins; 2. a public statement of one's beliefs

confound: to make someone else confused or mixed up

congregation (kahng-gruh-*gay*-shun):

an assembly; a group of people meeting together

consecrate (*kahn*-suh-krait): to set someone or something apart for a holy use—**consecrated**

consolation (kahn-suh-*lay*-shun): comfort; relief from a burden or from the loss of a loved one

contentions (kun-*ten*-chunz): arguments; discord

contentious (kun-*ten*-chuss): *adj.* quarrelsome

conversation (kahn-ver-*say*-shuŋ): 1. talk or discussion; 2. one's conduct or behavior

conversion (kun-*ver*-zhun): the act of changing from one thing to another, for example,

when a person turns away from a sinful life and accepts Christ as Savior

convert (kun-*vert*): *v.* to change something or someone from one thing to another; to win over

convert (*kahn*-vert): *n.* the person who has changed

Corinth: the capital city of Achaia, situated on the isthmus of Greece, about 50 miles west of Athens. It was one of the largest, richest, and most important cities of the Roman Empire, with a population estimated at 400,000. It was located on a principal trade route, and the commerce of the world passed through its harbors. It was a city of great immorality. Paul started a church there (Acts 18:1-18). He wrote two letters to the church—1 and 2 Corinthians.

Jesus Christ (Matthew 27, Luke 23)

Corinthian (kor-*in*-thee-un): a native or inhabitant of the Greek city of Corinth

corn: in Bible times, this meant grain of any kind. Corn such as we have was unknown.

Cornelius (kor-*neel*-yus): a Roman centurion in Caesarea; a kind and devout man. Baptized by Peter, he was the first Gentile to become a Christian (Acts 10).

cornet (kor-*net*): a musical instrument made from the horn of a ram or goat

corruption (kur-*rup*-shun): the ruining of that which is good and right; decay

council (*kown*-sul): a group of people who gather together to think about and discuss issues. The Sanhedrin was a Jewish council that discussed issues dealing with the law.

counsel (*kown*-sul): v. to give advice to someone; to talk things over

counsel: n. helpful advice from someone wise or older

countenance (*kownt*-en-unss): one's expression; the look on one's face

countervail (*kownt*-er-vail): to compensate; to exert force against a bad or harmful opposing force

court: an area of ground partly or completely closed in by walls or buildings

covenant (*kuv*-uh-nunt): a serious agreement or promise between two or more people or groups

covet (*kuv*-et): to greatly want something that belongs to another

covetousness (*kuv*-et-us-ness): selfish greed; envy

craft: 1. skill in making something; 2. skill in deceiving or tricking someone

Crete (kreet): the fourth largest island in the Mediterranean Sea. It lies southeast of Greece and is about 160 miles long and six to 35 miles wide. Cretans were in Jerusalem on the Day of Pentecost (Acts 2:11). A church was founded on the island (Titus 1:5-14). Fair Havens, where Paul's ship took refuge in a storm, was on this island (Acts 27:8).

Cretes, Cretans (kreets, kree-tunz): people living on the island of Crete, located in the Mediterranean Sea between Europe and Asia Minor.

Crispus (*kris*-pus): chief ruler of the Jewish synagogue in Corinth. After listening to Paul, he and his family became Christians (Acts 18:8). Crispus was personally baptized by Paul (1 Corinthians 1:14).

cross: two pieces of wood nailed together and used as a death punishment by the Romans. The person that was punished was nailed to the crossed pieces.

crucify (kroo-suh-fye): to kill someone by nailing him to a cross—n. **crucifixion**

cubit (kyoo-bit): a measure of length, the distance from the elbow to the tip of the middle finger (about 18 inches)

cummin, cumin: a low plant of the carrot family, having fragrant seeds, often used to check bleeding

cummin

cupbearer: a servant who filled a cup when a drink was served. The king's cupbearer first tasted the drink to see that it was not poisoned.

curse: to call upon God to send harm or death; to wish harm or evil upon someone

Cush: the oldest son of Ham, and grandson of Noah (Genesis 10:6-8)

custom (kus-tum): 1. the normal way of doing something, a practice of long standing; 2. taxes placed on goods brought into a country

cymbals (sim-bulz): a kind of musical instrument, consisting of two brass plates that were struck together

cypress: a kind of evergreen tree

Cyprus: the third largest island in the Mediterranean. It was about 43 miles south of the coast of Cilicia and 60 miles west of Syria. The island is about 145 miles long and 40 miles wide. It is rich in copper deposits. The gospel was preached there after Stephen was stoned (Acts 11:19, 20), and later by Paul and Barnabas (Acts 13:4), and by Barnabas and Mark (Acts 15:39). Also called Chittim or Kittim (Ezekiel 27:6).

Cyrene (sye-ree-nih): a city in northern Africa about halfway between Carthage and Alexandria. Simon, a man from Cyrene, was compelled by Roman soldiers to carry the cross for Jesus (Matthew 27:32). Cyrenians joined with Libertines, or Freedmen, and others in forming a synagogue in Jerusalem (Acts 6:9). Men from Cyrene early accepted Christianity and preached the gospel (Acts 11:20; 13:1).

Cyrenian (sye-ree-nee-un): person from the Libyan city of Cyrene, west of Egypt.

Cyrenius (sye-ree-nee-us): Roman governor of Syria (Luke 2:2). *Quirinius* is the Latin name and *Cyrenius*, the Greek.

Cyrus (sye-rus): Cyrus began the great Persian Empire that lasted until the time of Alexander the Great. He was a wise king and permitted the captive Jews in Babylon to return to their homeland and rebuild the temple (2 Chronicles 36:22, 23; Ezra 1:1-7; 5:13, 14).

Daniel (Daniel 6)

Dd

Dalmatia (dal-*may*-shuh): mountainous province on eastern shore of Adriatic Sea. Titus was sent here to preach the gospel (2 Timothy 4:10).

Damascus (duh-*mas*-kus): a city of Syria. Important trade routes went from the city to Egypt, Arabia, and Mesopotamia. It was mentioned as early as the time of Abraham (Genesis 14:15). David captured the city (2 Samuel 8:5, 6; 1 Chronicles 18:3-6). Various rulers had a part in the history of Israel and Judah (1 Kings 11:23-25; 15:16-21; 19:15; 20:34). In NT times, many Jews lived in the city and supported several synagogues (Acts 9:2). Paul was converted in Damascus (Acts 9:1-18). Later he was let down over the wall of the city to escape the fury of the Jews (Acts 9:24, 25).

damnation: being forever separated from God and suffering great punishment in Hell

Dan: the most northern city of Palestine. Jeroboam of Israel placed a golden calf in Dan for the people to worship (1 Kings 12:28-30).

Dan: the fifth son of Jacob, the first by Bilhah, Rachel's handmaid (Genesis 30:5, 6). His family began the tribe of Dan. The tribe acted as the rear guard during the exodus from Egypt (Numbers 10:25).

Daniel (*dan*-yul): a well-known prophet from the tribe of Judah. As a young man, he was taken to Babylon with other captives in 605 B.C. Daniel and three of his friends were respected and trained for the king's service (Daniel 1:3-7). Later, Daniel became one of the three presidents of the kingdom. Jealousy of Daniel led to a plot against him. He was thrown into a lions' den but God kept him unharmed (Daniel 6). A book bearing his name is among the books of prophecy in the OT.

Darius (duh-rye-us): leader of the Persian army that overthrew Babylon. Darius the Mede ruled in Babylon until Cyrus took over (Daniel 5:31; 6:28). He put 120 princes in charge of the kingdom, who would be ruled by presidents, Daniel being one of these.

dates: a fruit that grew on a kind of palm tree, one of the main foods for the people of Jesus' day

David: the eighth and youngest son of Jesse. He was a shepherd and lived in Bethlehem. Samuel anointed him to be the second king of Israel (1 Samuel 16:1, 10-13). David played the harp for King Saul (1 Samuel 16:23). He killed Goliath (1 Samuel 17:45-51). David and Jonathan, Saul's son, became dear friends (1 Samuel 18:1-4). Jealous King Saul tried to kill David but failed (1 Samuel 18—22). After the death of Saul, David became the second and greatest king of Israel.

day: For the Jews, the day began at sunset and ended at sunset.

Day of Atonement: the day, once a year, on which the high priest entered into the Most Holy Place and made atonement for the sins of the people—see **atonement**

deacon (dee-kun): a servant; someone set aside in the church with a special job to do

Dead Sea: a body of water in the Jordan Valley in southern Palestine about 47 miles long and about ten miles wide. It has the earth's lowest surface, 1,292 feet below sea level, and it measures over 1,000 feet at its deepest point. It is fed principally by the Jordan River. It has no outlet, and the salt and potash deposits have become more concentrated than in any other sea or lake in the world. The density of the water is so great that it is impossible for a person to sink. In the Scriptures it was called the Salt Sea (Genesis 14:3; Numbers 34:12), Sea of the Plain or Arabah (Deuteronomy 3:17), and the East Sea (Ezekiel 47:18; Joel 2:20).

dearth (derth): a lack of something; scarcity; a famine

Deborah: 1. Rebekah's nurse, who went with her to Palestine (Genesis 24:59; 35:8); 2. the fourth judge of Israel; a prophetess; wife of Lapidoth. She encouraged Barak, and they saved Israel from the Canaanites, who had been put down by Joshua but had become powerful again (Judges 4, 5).

debt (det): 1. something that one person owes another, like money or an obligation to do something; 2. sin

Decapolis (dee-kap-uh-lis): a region that began on the western side of the Jordan River where the Plain of Esdraelon opens out into the Jordan Valley, and stretched east across the Jordan encompassing the area that had been given to the tribe of Manasseh (Numbers 32:33-42). The area was dominated by a league of ten cities

the Dead Sea

populated by Greeks who had come in the wake of Alexander's conquest. They were established after the Romans occupied the area (65 B.C.). The ten cities were: Hippos, Scythopolis (Beth-shan), Damascus, Philadelphia, Gerasa, Dion, Gadara, Raphana, Pella, and Canatha. Other towns were added to the league later until there was a total of eighteen. Three roads connected Esdraelon with the commercial highway that ran between Damascus and Arabia. The ten towns were situated on these three roads and the highway. Many from Decapolis followed Jesus in His early ministry (Matthew 4:25). Jesus healed the Gadarene in this region (Mark 5:20).

decease (dih-*seess*): death

decree: a law; something ordered by one or more persons in authority

defile: to make something unclean or impure; to contaminate

Delilah (dee-*lye*-luh): a beautiful Philistine woman Samson loved, and to whom he revealed the secret of his strength. This brought him to disaster (Judges 16:4-21).

deliverance (dih-*lih*-ver-unss): being set free; rescue

Demas (*dee*-mus): a faithful helper of Paul while he was in prison in Rome (Colossians 4:14). Later he deserted Paul and went to Thessalonica (2 Timothy 4:10).

Demetrius (dih-*mee*-tree-us): 1. a silver-smith in Ephesus, who started a riot against Paul for preaching against his profitable business of making silver images of the goddess Diana (Acts 19:23-27); 2. a Christian praised by John (3 John 12)

demon: an evil spirit

demoniac (dih-*mo*-nee-ak): a person subject to the power of demons. Demons could cause a person to be deaf, mute, epileptic, mentally ill, or physically ill.

denarius (dih-*nar*-ee-us): a Roman coin

Derbe (*der*-bee): a city in Asia Minor in the southeastern corner of Lycaonia on the main road from Lystra to Laranda. On Paul's first missionary journey, he made many converts there (Acts 14:6, 20). He passed through Derbe on his second journey traveling from Cilicia to Lystra (Acts 16:1). Gaius, one of Paul's companions, was from Derbe (Acts 20:4).

desert: a hot, dry, barren land where few people live

despise (dih-*spize*): 1. to look down on something; 2. to treat something as worthless.

Devil: another name for Satan. He is the chief enemy of God and man. The devil tempts people to sin and tries to undo the work of God. On the Judgment Day he and his followers will be cast into Hell to remain there forever.

devour (dih-*vowr*): to eat up greedily; to seize and consume

didst: did

Didymus (*did*-uh-mus): see **Thomas**

diligent (*dil*-uh-jent): with great effort, care, and perseverance

Dinah: a daughter of Jacob and Leah (Genesis 30:21)

disciple (dis-*sipe*-ul) a learner; one who accepts the teachings of his master. Jesus had many disciples, some of whom later became His apostles.

discreet (dis-*kreet*): knowing when to speak and when to remain silent; knowing not to say too much—*n.* **discretion** (dis-*kreh*-shun)

dispensation (dis-pen-*say*-shun): an arrangement, plan, or order of things

dissension (dis-*sen*-shun): disagreement; quarreling or arguing over a matter

distaff: the part of a spinning wheel that held the wool or other material that was to be spun

divers: different, various

divination (div-in-*ay*-shun): the practice of foretelling future events

divine: heavenly; belonging to or having to do with God

doctor: in Jesus' day, a teacher of the law; they usually taught in public places such as the temple

doctrine (*dahk*-trin): teachings; something that is taught

Doeg (*do*-eg): an Edomite herdsman who served King Saul. When David was fleeing from Saul, he received help from the high priest at Nob. Doeg reported this to King Saul, and all of the priests, except one who escaped, were put to death (1 Samuel 21; 22).

doest, dost: do

doeth, doth: does

dominion (duh-*min*-yun): supreme power or authority

Dorcas (*dor*-kus): a Christian woman living in Joppa. She was well-known for her help to the poor. Peter raised her from the dead (Acts 9:36-43). She is also called *Tabitha*.

Dothan, Dothain, Dothaim (*do*-thun, *do*-thum): a town not far from Shechem and Samaria, near a caravan route. In this vicinity the brothers of Joseph cast him into a pit and then decided to sell him to a caravan of merchants going to Egypt (Genesis 37). When Elisha was in Dothan, Ben-Hadad, king of Syria, sent his armies to besiege the city (2 Kings 6:8-23).

dowry (*dow*-ree): 1. the money or goods that a bride gave to her husband when they were married; 2. the money or goods that a husband gave to the father of the bride

draught (draft): 1. the act of drawing a fishing net from the water; 2. a catch of fish; 3. a toilet or sink

dress: to prepare something for use or service

drove: 1. a group of animals moving or being driven along together; 2. a group of people moving along together

Drusilla (droo-*sill*-uh): daughter of Herod Agrippa I; wife of Felix, governor of Judea, before whom Paul was brought at Caesarea (Acts 24:24, 25)

dulcimer (*dul*-suh-mur): a musical instrument; the modern dulcimer is a box strung with fifty wires from 18 to 36 inches long, and played with two small hammers.

dulcimer

dungeon (*dun*-jun): a dark underground place in which prisoners were kept

dwell: to stay or reside in one place—*past tense,* **dwelt.**

dye: *n.* a liquid used to add color to something, or to change its color.

dye: *v.* to change the color of something using dye.

Eutychus (Acts 20)

Ee

Ebal (ee-bul): a mountain in the central part of Canaan. It is the highest point in Samaria, being 3,077 feet high. It is separated from Mount Gerizim by a narrow valley, and lies north of Shechem. Jacob's well was at its foot (John 4:20). When the Israelites first entered Canaan, Joshua erected on Mount Ebal a monument of stones on which the law was written, and a stone altar. The tribes were divided, with half on Mount Gerizim and half on Mount Ebal, and the law with its blessings and curses was recited by the people antiphonally, the blessings coming from Mount Gerizim and the curses from Mount Ebal (Deuteronomy 27:4-26; Joshua 8:30-35).

Ebed-melech (ee-bed-mee-lik): an Ethiopian eunuch in the palace of Zedekiah. He drew Jeremiah up out of the dungeon (Jeremiah 38:7-13). For this deed, God, through Jeremiah, assured him safety in the coming destruction of the city (Jeremiah 39:15-18).

Eden: a place where God planted the garden in which He put Adam and Eve. They lived there until they sinned and were sent away (Genesis 2, 3). Eden's location is unknown, although some thought it was in the area of Babylon where the Tigris and Euphrates Rivers come close together.

edify (ed-uh-fye): to build up and make strong; to instruct or improve in spiritual matters—n. **edification**

Edom (ee-dum): a rugged mountainous territory south of the Dead Sea. One of the highest points of Edom was Mount Hor, where Aaron was buried (Numbers 20:27, 28). Esau first settled the country (Genesis 25:25-30; 36:1, 8), and his descendants, the Edomites, inhabited the region. The country was also called Seir or Mount Seir.

Edomites (ee-dum-ites): a Semitic people descended from Esau. They settled in the south of Palestine and across Jordan. They became the Idumeans in NT times (Mark 3:8).

Egypt: a country in the northeastern section of Africa. The Nile River flows the length of the country, and without its watering, Egypt would be a barren desert. The Nile valley and delta are bound by desert. Just north of the city of Cairo the delta spreads out to a shape about 125 miles long and 115 miles wide. The fertile land of Goshen, where the Israelites lived while they were in bondage in Egypt, was in the eastern part of this area (Exodus 1—14). In the time of the OT, Egypt was a powerful empire. During the time of the NT, it was a cultural center and provided grain to the Roman Empire. Jesus lived in Egypt while He was a young child (Matthew 2:13, 19-21). People from Egypt were present in Jerusalem on the Day of Pentecost (Acts 2:10).

Ehud (ee-hud): second judge of Israel, son of Gera of the tribe of Benjamin. He was left-handed. He delivered his people from the oppression of Eglon, king of Moab. After that the land had peace for 80 years (Judges 3:5-30).

Elam (ee-lum): a country in southwestern Asia on the east side of the Tigris River across from Babylonia. Susa was its capital. Ezra 4:9 mentions that people from Elam were brought to Samaria by the Assyrians.

elder: 1. the father or head of a family or tribe; 2. a leader in the church; bishop; pastor; 3. an older person

Eleazar (el-ee-ay-zer): 1. third son of Aaron (Exodus 6:23). At the death of Aaron, Eleazar became the high priest (Numbers 20:28). He helped Moses in numbering the people (Numbers 26:1-4). He helped Joshua divide the promised land among the tribes (Numbers 34:17); 2. one of the three mighty men in David's army (2 Samuel 23:9)

elect: v. to choose

elect: n. chosen or selected people

Eli (ee-lye): a descendant of Aaron; judge of Israel and high priest at Shiloh. He trained Samuel to be the religious leader of Israel (1 Samuel 1:28; 2:11). Eli had one great weakness; he did not deal firmly with his wicked sons, Hophni and Phinehas. Eli was 98 years old when he died (1 Samuel 3:13; 4).

Eliab (ee-lye-ub): son of Jesse and oldest brother of David (1 Samuel 17:12, 13)

Eliezer (el-ih-ee-zer): 1. servant of Abraham (Genesis 15:2); 2. second son of Moses and Zipporah (Exodus 18:4)

Elijah (ee-lye-juh): one of the greatest prophets. He prophesied during the reigns of Ahab and Ahaziah. Elijah was fed by ravens during a famine sent to punish the sinful people (1 Kings 17:1-7). He met with prophets of Baal on Mt. Carmel and defeated them with God's help (1 Kings 18). Jezebel tried to have him killed. He was taken up to Heaven by a chariot of fire in a whirlwind (2 Kings 2:9-12). Elisha carried on his work.

Elim (ee-lim): the site of Israel's second encampment after crossing the Red Sea (Exodus 15:27; Numbers 33:9). This place offered refreshment from 12 wells and 70 palms, unlike the bitter waters of Marah, their first encampment (Exodus 15:23-26).

Elimelech (ee-lim-uh-lek): husband of Naomi. They left Judah because of a famine and moved to Moab, where Elimelech died (Ruth 1:1-3).

Elisabeth (ee-liz-uh-beth): wife of Zechariah and mother of John the Baptist. She was a relative of Mary, the mother of Jesus (Luke 1:5-64).

Elisha (ee-lye-shuh): son of Shaphat. God appointed him to succeed Elijah as a prophet in the northern kingdom (1 Kings 19:16-19). Elisha saw the chariot of fire that took Elijah into Heaven (2 Kings 2:11, 12). He had a long ministry during the reigns of Jehoram, Jehu, Jehoahaz, and Joash. The healing of Naaman's leprosy was one of his many miracles (2 Kings 5).

Elkanah (el-kay-nuh): father of Samuel (1 Samuel 1:1, 2)

Elohim (el-oh-heem): the Hebrew name used most often for God

Elymas (el-ih-mus): a Jewish imposter, Bar-jesus by name, who pretended to learn the future by sorcery. Paul struck him with temporary blindness (Acts 13:6-12).

emerald: a precious green gem

Emmanuel (ee-man-yoo-el): "God with us;" Isaiah used this name in reference to Jesus

Emmaus (em-may-us): a town about seven miles from Jerusalem. On the Sunday when Jesus arose from the dead, He appeared to two men walking from Jerusalem to Emmaus (Luke 24:13-35).

endeavor (en-dev-ur): v. to attempt or try to do something

endeavor: n. the effort spent in trying to reach a goal

endure: to last a long time without weakening or failing

En-gedi (en—gee-dye): an agricultural settlement watered by a spring on the western shore of the Dead Sea about midway between the northern and southern ends of the sea, in the territory of Judah (Joshua 15:62). When David was fleeing from Saul, David and his men hid in a cave in this region while Saul slept nearby (1 Samuel 23:29—24:22).

enmity (en-muh-tee): hatred or hostility between two enemies

Enoch (ee-nuk): 1. the oldest son of Cain (Genesis 4:17, 18); 2. the son of Jared, and the father of Methuselah (Genesis 5:18-21). Enoch "walked with God," and he was taken up into Heaven without dying (Genesis 5:24; Hebrews 11:5).

ensign (en-sun or en-sine): a long pole with a flag, design, or emblem of a group of people or a nation

envy (en-vee): v. to be jealous of someone because of a possession or talent that he has

envy: n. jealousy

Epaphras (ep-uh-frus): a Christian in the church at Colossae, perhaps its minister. While Paul was a prisoner in Rome, Epaphras brought him a good account of the church (Colossians 1:7, 8; 4:12). He remained in Rome, "Paul's fellow prisoner" (Philemon 23).

Epaphroditus (ee-paf-ro-dye-tus): a companion of Paul highly recommended by him (Philippians 2:25-30). He was delegated by the church in Philippi to take their love gift to Paul, who was in prison in Rome (Philippians 4:18).

Ephesian (ee-fee-zhun): 1. a native or inhabitant of Ephesus, the capital city of the Roman province of Asia; 2. the title of the letter Paul wrote to the Christians in Ephesus.

Ephesus (ef-uh-sus): a city of Lydia, in western Asia Minor, at the mouth of the Cayster River, halfway between Melitus and Smyrna, on an important trade route. It was the capital of the Roman province of Asia. Because of its fine harbor and roads coming into the city, Ephesus, with more than 300,000 population, became the commercial center of Roman Asia. The city was well-known for its temple to Diana (Artemis). Many Jews with Roman citizenship lived in the city. Paul visited here a short time toward the end of his second missionary journey (Acts 18:19-21). On his third journey, he spent almost three years in Ephesus (Acts 19). Timothy spent time in this city helping the church leaders (1 and 2 Timothy).

ephod (ee-fahd): a tunic of fine linen embroidered in gold, blue, purple, and scarlet thread, worn by the high priest

Ephraim (ee-free-um): 1. younger son of Joseph and Asenath, an Egyptian woman (Genesis 41:52). Jacob, their grandfather, gave him and his brother Manasseh a blessing (Genesis 48:8-14). Founder of one of the tribes of Israel; 2. the central hill country of Palestine given to the tribes of Ephraim and Manasseh, although half the tribe of Manasseh settled east of the Jordan River (Numbers 32:33, 39-42). It is sometimes called Mount Ephraim; 3. a city about five miles northeast of Bethel and about 15 miles from Jerusalem. Jesus came into this area after Lazarus was raised from the dead (John 11:47-54).

Ephrath (*ef*-ruth): shorter form of Ephratah or Ephrathah, the region around Bethlehem (Micah 5:2). Rachel was buried in this area (Genesis 35:16).

Ephron (*ee*-frun): a Hittite from whom Abraham bought the field and cave of Machpelah in which he buried his wife Sarah (Genesis 23:7-20)

epistle (ee-*pis*-ul): a letter

Erastus (ee-*ras*-tus): a friend of Paul (Acts 19:22). This friend may be the same Erastus who was the treasurer of the city of Corinth. He sent greetings to the Christians at Rome (Romans 16:23).

Esau (*ee*-saw): first twin son of Isaac and Rebekah (Genesis 25:25). He became a hunter (Genesis 25:27). He sold his birthright to his twin brother, Jacob (Genesis 25:29-34). Jacob deceived their father in order to receive the special blessing that rightfully belonged to Esau, the firstborn, but Esau later forgave him (Genesis 33:1-12).

eschew (es-*choo*): to shun; to avoid or stay away from something such as a bad habit

Esdraelon (ez-dray-ee-lun): the fertile plain of central Palestine, watered by the Kishon River. It lies between Galilee on the north and Samaria on the south. It was the site of some important battles in Jewish history (Judges 4; 1 Samuel 31; 2 Kings 23:29). Called the Plain or Valley of Jezreel in the OT

Eshtaol (*esh*-tay-ol): one of the 14 cities occupying the foothills of Judah (Joshua 15:33). It was about 13 miles northwest of Jerusalem. Samson was buried near here (Judges 16:31).

espoused (es-*powzd*): betrothed; to be promised to someone in marriage or engaged to marry someone

estate (es-*tait*): 1. state or condition; 2. possessions or property

Esther (*es*-ter): a beautiful Jewish girl who became the wife of Ahasuerus, king of Persia. She and her cousin, Mordecai, overcame a plot to destroy the Jews (book of Esther). Her Jewish name was Hadassah.

eternal: everlasting; having no beginning and no end; timeless

Ethiopia (ee-thee-*oh*-pee-uh): a country in Africa, located south of Egypt. The border between Egypt and Ethiopia was Syene, which is modern Aswan, at the first cataract of the Nile River. The southern border was indefinite but was probably about 1,000 miles south of Syene. This country, or a part of it, was sometimes called Cush. The people of Ethiopia had skin of different appearance (Jeremiah 13:23). Moses married an Ethiopian woman (Numbers 12:1). Ethiopians came against Judah (2 Chronicles 12:3; 14:9-13; 16:7-9; 2 Kings 19:9).

Eunice (*yoo*-nis): a devout Jewish woman and mother of Timothy (Acts 16:1; 2 Timothy 1:5).

eunuch (*yoo*-nuk): a man who had an operation that weakened his sexual desires and made it impossible for him to father children. Eunuchs often held high positions and had great authority in the households of rulers.

Euodias (yoo-*oh*-dee-us): see **Syntyche**

Euphrates (yoo-*fray*-teez): the largest river in western Asia. It rises in the mountains of Armenia (eastern Turkey) and flows about 1,675 miles to join the Tigris River. It flows in a southeastern course to the Persian Gulf. The Euphrates was one of the rivers of the Garden of Eden (Genesis 2:14). The promise to Abraham stated that his inheritance should reach the Euphrates (Genesis 15:18; Deuteronomy 1:7; Joshua 1:4). Near the banks of the river were such great cities as Carchemish, Mari, Babylon, and Ur.

Eutychus (*yoo*-tih-kus): a young man of Troas who fell asleep while Paul was preaching. He fell from the third floor window to his death. Paul restored his life (Acts 20:9-12).

evangelist: a preacher or messenger who takes the good news about Jesus to others

Eve: the first woman. God caused a deep sleep to come upon Adam, and removed one of his ribs. From this rib, God made a wife, or "helpmeet," for Adam. Adam called her name Eve, for she was the mother of all living (Genesis 3:20). Eve committed the first sin in the world, eating the fruit from the tree that God had forbidden and giving some to Adam also. As a part of their punishment, God sent them out of the Garden of Eden. Eve was the mother of Cain, Abel, and Seth, as well as other sons and daughters (Genesis 2; 3; 4:1, 2, 25, 26; 5:1-5).

even: evening; time between sunset and bedtime

everlasting: eternal; without end

exalt (eks-ahlt): to lift up; to glorify; to praise or show great respect to someone or something

exhort (eks-*ort*): to urge; to get a person to do something by giving advice or warnings—n. **exhortation**

eyewitness: 1. a person who sees something happen; 2. a person who gives a report on what he has seen

Ezekiel (ee-*zeek*-yul): one of the OT prophets. He was taken captive from Jerusalem to Babylon. Although an exile in a foreign land, Ezekiel was free to prophesy. He is the writer of the book of Ezekiel in the OT

Ezra: a Jewish priest and scribe who was with the exiles in Babylon. With the permission of King Artaxerxes, he returned to Jerusalem to carry out religious reform. Several years later he helped Nehemiah with the dedication of the wall and took part in reading the law of Moses to the people (book of Ezra; Nehemiah 8).

Paul appears before Felix (Acts 24)

Ff

fable: a fictitious or made-up story that is told to teach a lesson

Fair Havens: a small bay on the southern coast of Crete. The bay was protected on the southwest by two small islands. Paul urged the owner of the ship carrying him to Rome to remain in Fair Havens for the winter (Acts 27:8-12). Ancient ships did not usually sail on the Mediterranean Sea during the stormy months of November to March.

faith: a firm belief or trust in a person or thing; belief in what God says, even though one cannot see or understand everything

false witness: lying or making an untrue statement, usually in court

famine (*fam*-in): a great shortage of food, usually caused by a long period without rain

farthing: a small coin worth very little

fast: *v.* to go without food for a certain period of time

fast: *n.* the time during which you go without food

fathom: a unit of length equal to six feet

fear: 1. a feeling of wonder and deep respect and love, as for God; awe; 2 a sense of being afraid

feast: 1. a celebration with much food; 2. a religious celebration (see chart, p. 44)

Felix: a wicked and cruel Roman ruler of Judea, appointed by the emperor Claudius and recalled by Nero. Paul was brought to trial before Felix in Caesarea. Felix kept Paul in prison for two years in the hope of gaining bribe money from him (Acts 23, 24).

Feasts of the Jews

Name	English Month	Duration of Feast	What it Commemorated	Main Feature of its Observance	Other Names
Passover	April	One Week	Passing over of death; departure from Egypt	Eating the paschal lamb	Unleavened Bread
Pentecost	June	One Day	Giving the law at Mt. Sinai	Offering two loaves, representing first-fruits of wheat	Weeks Firstfruits
Tabernacles	October	One Week	Life in the wilderness	Living in booths	Ingathering
Trumpets	October	One Day	New Year's Day	Blowing of trumpets	
Dedication	December	Eight Days	Rededication of the temple	Rejoicing, singing, lighting of lamps and torches	Lights
Purim	March	Two Days	Queen Esther's rescue of the Jews	Reading the book of Esther	

fellowship: partnership; sharing; the coming together of friends who are interested in the same things

festival: a special time set apart for a religious celebration

Festus: the Roman governor whom Nero appointed to succeed Felix as a ruler of Judea. Paul presented his defense before Festus, King Agrippa II, and Bernice (Acts 25, 26).

fig: a kind of fruit, eaten either fresh or dried

firmament (fur-muh-ment): the whole sky above; the heavens

firstborn: the first child born in a family

firstfruit: the first of a crop gathered at the time of harvest, offered to God to thank Him for the harvest

fish gate: one of the gates in the wall around Jerusalem. The fish market was probably near this gate.

flags: a plant that grows along rivers and in marshy places

flail: a wooden stick used in threshing, to separate grain from the chaff

fleece: a sheep's coat of wool

flesh: 1. skin and muscles, of either man

or animal; 2. mankind, or all living creatures; 3. the physical part of man, rather than the spiritual

flock: 1. a large group of sheep or birds; 2. a group of people, like a church congregation, being guided by a leader

foolish: being without good judgment, especially about what is right and wrong; acting in a way that brings about sin

forasmuch (*for*-uz-much): since

forbear: 1. to do without something; abstain; 2. to have patience; to control yourself even when wronged or provoked

foreigner: a person living in a country not his own

forerunner: someone who comes first, to make ready for the coming of another

forgive: 1. to pardon; to stop being angry about a wrong thing someone has done to you, and to forget about it; 2. to excuse someone from having to pay a debt he owes you

fornication (for-nih-*kay*-shun): sexual relations between unmarried persons

forsake: to give up or abandon

forthwith: right away; immediately

fortify: to make something stronger, for defense—*n.* **fortification**

fountain: a spring of water; a source, or a place where water comes from

fourfold: four times as great or as many

fowl: any kind of bird

frankincense: an expensive perfume that was burned to make a pleasant odor. It was used in the worship ceremony of the Israelites, and also as medicine; see **incense**

frontlet: a small leather case worn on the forehead and tied with a ribbon, which contained part of the OT law. These were worn by Jewish men as a show of their religion

frontlet

fugitive (*fyoo*-jit-iv): someone who runs away from something, often from the law or from justice

fulfill: to complete; to do what is required; to satisfy

furlong: a unit of length, equal to 220 yards or 1/8 mile

furrow: the row of soil turned up by the action of a plow

Goliath (1 Samuel 17)

Gg

Gabriel (*gay*-bree-el): an angel of high rank sent to interpret a vision of the prophet Daniel (Daniel 8:16-27). Gabriel also announced the birth of John the Baptist to Zechariah (Luke 1:11-22) and announced the birth of Jesus to Mary (Luke 1:26-38).

Gad: 1. the seventh son of Jacob, by Zilpah, Leah's handmaid (Genesis 30:9-11). He was the leader of one of the 12 tribes of Israel; 2. a prophet of King David. He helped to arrange the musical services of the temple (2 Chronicles 29:25) and wrote the acts of David in a book (1 Chronicles 29:29).

Gadara (*gad*-uh-ruh): a city of the Decapolis, located near the southeastern end of the Sea of Galilee. A strategic road from Tiberias to Damascus went through Gadara. Another road branched off to go all the way to the Gulf of Persia. Jesus healed a demo-niac near Gadara (Mark 5:1-19; Luke 8:26-37).

gainsay: to speak against; to deny or contradict

Gaius (*gay*-us): 1. a man of Macedonia. A companion of Paul who was dragged into a theater during a riot in Ephesus (Acts 19:23-30); 2. a man of Derbe who went with Paul on his last journey to Asia (Acts 20:4); 3. a man of Corinth, baptized by Paul, who showed hospitality to his fellow Christians (Romans 16:23; 1 Corinthians 1:14)

Galatia (guh-*lay*-shee-uh): originally Galatia was a territory where the Gauls settled in the north central region of Asia Minor. About 25 B.C. Augustus made Galatia a Roman province, with Ancyra its capital. Its territory included parts of Pontus, Phrygia, Lycaonia, Pisidia, Paphlagonia, Isauria, as well as the old region of Galatia. Included in the province were the cities the apostle Paul visited on his first missionary journey (Acts 13, 14). Paul's use of the term Galatia (1 Corinthians 16:1; Galatians 1:2; 2 Timothy 4:10) and Peter's (1 Peter 1:2) probably refer to the whole province.

Galatian (guh-*lay*-shun): a native or inhabitant of Galatia, a province of Asia Minor. Paul wrote a letter to the churches in Galatia.

Galilean (gal-lih-*lee*-un): a native or inhabitant of the province of Galilee. Although Galilee and Judea were only 60 miles apart, the people differed in customs, and in pronunciation and accent of their speech.

Galilee: the most northern province of the three into which the Romans divided Palestine west of the Jordan River. It was about 60 miles long and 30 miles wide. The area is generally mountainous. Fruit and olive orchards grew on the hills, and grain and grass in the rich, fertile valleys. Roads came across Galilee from all directions and brought trade from Syria, Arabia, and Egypt. Jesus spent most of His ministry in this area (see map, p. 91).

Galilee, Sea of: a freshwater lake in northern Palestine fed by the Jordan River. It was also called Sea of Chinnereth (Numbers 34:11), Lake of Gennesaret (Luke 5:1), and Sea of Tiberias (John 6:1), all names taken from places on the western shores. The lake is about 13 miles long and 7½ miles wide. It lies about 682 feet below sea level, and has a depth of 80 to 150 feet. It is about 60 miles north of Jerusalem, and surrounded by hills, except where the Jordan enters and leaves the lake. The water is generally calm, but frequently sudden, violent storms rush down from the slopes of the mountains (Luke 8:22-25). Because of the abundance of fish in its waters, a great fishing business was carried on. Nine cities with a population of 15,000 or more bordered the lake. Three of the most important were Tiberias, Capernaum, and Bethsaida. On and around the Sea of Galilee Jesus performed miracles, taught, and called His apostles.

gall: 1. a bitter substance used to deaden pain; 2. anything that is bitter; 3. a poison

Gallio (*gal*-lee-oh): the Roman proconsul of Achaia when Paul was in Corinth. When the Jews brought Paul before him, Gallio refused to hear any charges against Paul and dismissed him (Acts 18:12-17).

Gamaliel (guh-*may*-lee-ul): a member of the Jewish Sanhedrin, a Pharisee, and a teacher of the law. Paul, when young, had been one of his students (Acts 5:34-39; 22:3).

garner: to gather grain in a field

Gath: one of the five great cities of the Philistines (1 Samuel 6:17). Gath was

the home of Goliath (1 Samuel 17:4). David fled from Saul to the king of Gath (1 Samuel 21:10-15).

Gath-hepher (gath—*hee*-fer): a town three miles northeast of Nazareth, on the border of Zebulun. It was the birthplace of Jonah (2 Kings 14:25).

Gaza (*gay*-zuh): the most southern of the five Philistine cities. The city was situated on the main road from Mesopotamia to Egypt, at the edge of the desert, and at the junction of a trade route from southern Arabia. Gaza was assigned to Judah by Joshua (Joshua 15:47; Judges 1:18). It was captured by the Philistines (Judges 13:1). Samson was put in prison and died in Gaza (Judges 16:1, 21, 30). Philip converted the Ethiopian eunuch on the road to Gaza (Acts 8:26).

Gedaliah (ged-uh-*lye*-uh): a man of Judah who was appointed by Nebuchadnezzar to be governor of the people left in Judah after the capture of Jerusalem (2 Kings 25:22).

Gehazi (guh-*hay*-zye): the servant of Elisha (2 Kings 4:8-37; 5:20; 8:4).

generation (jen-er-*ay*-shun): 1. the action of producing children; 2. each step along the line of descent from an ancestor; 3. the span of time between the birth of parents and the birth of their children

Gennesaret, Lake of (guh-*ness*-uh-ret): see **Galilee, Sea of**

Gentile (*jen*-tile): people or nations that are not Jewish

Gerizim (guh-*rye*-zim, *gehr*-ih-zim): a

the Sea of Galilee

steep rocky mountain of Samaria in central Palestine facing Mount Ebal on the northern side of the valley in which the city of Shechem was located. When the Israelites conquered central Palestine, Joshua placed half the tribes on Mount Gerizim to read the blessings of the law and half on Mount Ebal across the valley to pronounce the curses (Deuteronomy 11:29; 27:12, 13; Joshua 8:33-35). The Samaritans built a temple on the mountain. They still worshiped there in Jesus' day (John 4:7-26).

Gershom (ger-shum): the first son of Moses and Zipporah (Exodus 18:3)

Gethsemane (geth-sem-uh-nee): a garden, probably of olive trees, with a press to squeeze oil from the fruit. It was east of Jerusalem, a short distance beyond the brook Kidron. Jesus prayed in agony in the garden, and He was arrested there (Matthew 26:36-56; Mark 14:32-52; Luke 22:39-54; John 18:1-12).

Gibeah, Gibeath (gib-ee-uh, gib-ee-uth): a town of Benjamin about four miles north of Jerusalem. Saul lived in Gibeah when he was anointed to be king (1 Samuel 10:17-26). Later it was his capital city (1 Samuel 11:4; 23:19).

Gibeon (gib-ee-un): a city of Benjamin located about six miles northwest of Jerusalem, near the intersection of three roads going to Joppa. At the time of the conquest of Canaan, Gibeon was the most important of four Hivite cities. By trickery, these cities made a treaty with Joshua, thus securing Israelite protection (Joshua 9). Solomon offered sacrifice at Gibeon and received a message from the Lord there (1 Kings 3:3-15).

Gideon (gid-ee-un): son of Joash of the tribe of Manasseh. A judge in Israel for 40 years. With God's help and an army of only 300 men he defeated the Midianites. Gideon was also called Jerubbaal (Judges 6, 7).

Gihon (gye-hahn): 1. the name given to one of the four rivers coming from the Garden of Eden (Genesis 2:13); 2. a spring outside the walls of Jerusalem, from which the city obtained part of its water supply (2 Chronicles 32:30; 33:14). Solomon was anointed king at Gihon (1 Kings 1:32-40).

Gilboa (gil-*bo*-uh): a range of hills on the east side of the Plain of Esdraelon. It forms the watershed between the Jordan and Kishon rivers. It is about eight miles long, curving to the southeast, then south to merge with the central uplands of Samaria. On the table-lands and gentle western slopes grow wheat, barley, figs, and olives, and pasture land can be found for grazing. The rest of the ridge of mountains is rock or covered with brushwood and wild grass. Saul was attacked by the Philistines on Mount Gilboa. His sons were killed in the battle. He was wounded and then fell on his sword and killed himself (1 Samuel 31:1-8; 1 Chronicles 10:1-8).

Gilead (*gil*-ee-ud): the land owned by Israel east of the Jordan River, extending from Bashan on the north, the Arabian desert on the east, and Moab and Ammon on the south. Jacob camped at Gilead when he fled from Laban (Genesis 31:7-47). Moses was permitted to see the promised land, including Gilead, before his death (Deuteronomy 34:1). When Absalom rebelled against David, he and his forces gathered in the land of Gilead (2 Samuel 17:26). The country was noted for its balm, a pale yellow fragrant resin taken from trees (Jeremiah 8:22; 46:11).

Gilgal (*gil*-gal): the first place the Israelites camped after crossing the Jordan River, and their headquarters during the conquest of Canaan (Joshua 4:19-24). It was about ten miles from the Jordan and about two miles from Jericho. Saul was made king at Gilgal (1 Samuel 11:15). There he later disobeyed God by offering his own sacrifice (1 Samuel 13:1-15). Some of the tribe of Judah met David at Gilgal when he returned after the death of Absalom (2 Samuel 19:15, 40).

gird: to dress; to put on clothes, especially for a certain purpose, like battle or traveling

girdle: a wide sash or belt

girdle

glean: to pick up the grain that falls on the ground and was left by the reapers during harvest

glorify: to praise; to give great honor

gnash (nash): to grit the teeth together in rage and anger

goad: a pointed rod or stick used to drive or urge on an animal

God: the supreme Creator and Ruler of everything in the universe. He was from the beginning and will be forever. He is the giver of all life, and by His power all life is sustained.

godhead: the three Persons of God; Father, Son, and Holy Spirit

godly; holy; faithful and devoted to God—n. **godliness**

gods: wood, stone, or metal idols or images, believed to be powerful by those who worship them

goest: go

goeth: goes

Goliath (guh-*lye*-uth): a giant of Gath, over nine feet tall, and a warrior of the Philistine army. He defied the armies of Israel. David met the challenge of this giant. Calling on the name of the Lord, David killed Goliath with his slingshot (1 Samuel 17).

Gomorrah (guh-*mahr*-uh): a city in the plain of the Jordan, probably on the southern shore of the Dead Sea (Genesis 13:10). The twin cities of Sodom and Gomorrah were both associated with great sin and wickedness. They were destroyed by fire from Heaven (Genesis 18:20; 19:24-28).

goodly: beautiful, handsome

Goshen (go-shun): 1. the territory in Egypt where Jacob and his family were permitted to settle (Genesis 47:6). It was located in the northeastern part of the Nile Delta. Joseph went to meet his father in Goshen (Genesis 46:28, 29). Jacob and his family greatly multiplied and were still in Goshen during their bondage (Exodus 8:22; 9:26); 2. a district in the southern part of Judah, between Gaza and Gibeon (Joshua 10:41); 3. a town in the hill country of Judah, 13 miles southwest of Hebron (Joshua 15:51).

gospel: 1. good news; the story of Jesus Christ—His birth, ministry, death, burial, and resurrection; 2. any of the first four books of the NT—Matthew, Mark, Luke, and John

governor: an appointed or elected official who had power over a certain area of land. In NT times, Rome appointed a governor to rule over the land of Palestine.

Gozan (go-zan): a town and district in Mesopotamia on the Habor River near the Euphrates River. It was one of the places to which Israelites from Samaria were deported when the northern kingdom fell to the Assyrians in 722 B.C. (2 Kings 17:1-6; 18:11; 19:12; 1 Chronicles 5:26).

grace: a great kindness that is not deserved

grave: a place of burial of a body

graveclothes: linen cloth in which the dead were wrapped before burial

graven image: an idol carved out of wood, stone, or metal

grieve (greev): to cause someone to suffer or to feel sorrow

grievous (*greev*-us): serious, painful

guile (gile): trickery; deceit

guiltless: innocent, without sin; free from the responsibility for sin

Haman (Esther 3—7)

Hh

Habakkuk (huh-*bak*-kuk): a prophet of Judah shortly before its fall. He wrote one of the books of the OT.

habitation (hab-uh-*tay*-shun): a place to live; residence

Habor: a river in Mesopotamia where captives from the ten northern tribes were taken after the siege of Samaria by the Assyrians (2 Kings 17:1-6)

Hadassah (huh-*das*-suh): see **Esther**

Hades (*hay*-deez): the place where the dead await the judgment

Hagar (*hay*-gar): an Egyptian woman, a maid of Sarah. Hagar was the mother of Abraham's son Ishmael (Genesis 16:1-16).

Haggai (*hag*-ee-eye): a prophet in Jerusalem after the return of the Israelites from exile in Babylon. His OT book concerns the rebuilding of the temple in Jerusalem.

Hai: see **Ai**

Halah (*hay*-luh): a district in the Assyrian Empire where many of the Israelites were taken when Samaria was captured (2 Kings 17:1-6; 18:11; 1 Chronicles 5:26)

hallelujah: see **alleluia**

hallowed (*hal*-ode or *hal*-oh-wed): 1. holy; sacred; set apart for God; 2. deeply loved and respected; honored

Ham: the youngest son of Noah. He and his wife were in the ark during the flood. From him descended the dark races (Genesis 6:10; 7:13; 10:6-20).

Haman (*hay*-mun): a high official in the court of Ahasuerus, king of Persia. He plotted to destroy the Jews but was discovered by Esther and Mordecai. Haman died on the gallows he had prepared for Mordecai (Esther 3—7).

Hanani (huh-*nay*-nye): a brother of Nehemiah. While Nehemiah was in exile, Hanani brought him the bad news of Jerusalem. Later Hanani and Hananiah, the ruler of the palace, were given charge of Jerusalem (Nehemiah 1:2, 3; 7:2).

Hananiah (han-uh-*nye*-uh): the name of 14 different men in the OT, most important of whom was the false prophet in Jeremiah's day (Jeremiah 28)

handmaid, handmaiden: a woman servant

Hannah: wife of Elkanah; mother of Samuel. She prayed for a son and vowed to devote him to the Lord's service. Her prayer was answered, and she took the boy to Eli, the priest. Samuel became a great prophet and the last of the judges (1 Samuel 1, 2).

Haran (*hair*-un): the third son of Terah and youngest brother of Abram; father of Lot (Genesis 11:26-28)

Haran (*hair*-un): a city in Mesopotamia. It was a commercial center about 240 miles northwest of Nineveh and about 280 miles northeast of Damascus. It was on one of the main trade routes between Babylon and the Mediterranean Sea. Abraham and Terah lived in this city for a time, and Terah died there (Genesis 11:31—12:5). Later

Abraham sent his servant there to find a wife for Isaac from among his relatives (Genesis 24:4). Isaac sent Jacob to the same area to search for a wife (Genesis 29:4).

harden: to become stubborn and unwilling to listen, as in "harden your hearts"

harlot (*har*-lut): 1. a woman who had sexual relations with a man in exchange for money; a prostitute; 2. someone who worshiped idols

Harosheth (huh-*ro*-sheth): a town on the northern bank of the Kishon River, about 16 miles northwest of Megiddo. Sisera, captain of Jabin's army, lived there (Judges 4:2).

harp: a musical instrument with strings

harvest: the gathering of grain or other crops after they have grown

hast: have

hath: has

haughty (*hawt*-ee): proud; scornful; acting superior toward others

Hazor (*hay*-zer): the capital city of the Canaanite kingdom in northern Palestine. It was ruled by Jabin. Joshua captured Hazor, killed Jabin, and burned the city (Joshua 11:1-13). Later another Jabin was king of Hazor, and he was subdued by Deborah and Barak (Judges 4). Hazor was located strategically on a trade route from Damascus to the Mediterranean, so Solomon fortified the city (1 Kings 9:15). Later, Israelites living in the city were taken captive to Assyria (2 Kings 15:29).

hearken (*har*-ken): to listen to something; to obey

heathen (*hee*-then): 1. a person who does not worship God; 2. one who is uncivilized or not religious; 3. a term used by the Jews to refer to the Gentiles (non-Jews)

Heaven: the place where God and His angels live; the everlasting home promised to those faithful to God

Heber (*hee*-ber): husband of Jael, who killed Sisera. He was of the Kenite tribe and a descendant of Moses' brother-in-law or father-in-law, Hobab (Judges 4:11-24).

Hebrew (*hee*-broo): 1. a Jew; one of the chosen people of God who were direct descendants of Abraham through Isaac; 2. the language of the Jews

Hebron (*hee*-brun): a city in the hill country of Judea located about 20 miles south-southwest of Jerusalem on the road to Beersheba. It is one of the oldest cities in the world. Abram lived in Mamre near Hebron (Genesis 13:18; 14:1-13; 18:1-15). Isaac lived at Hebron (Genesis 35:27). Jacob sent Joseph from this region to his brothers (Genesis 37:14). Abraham, Sarah, Isaac, Rebekah, Jacob, and Leah were

buried in the cave Abraham had purchased here (Genesis 23:1-9; 49:31; 50:4-13). The 12 spies saw Hebron (Numbers 13:21, 22). Hebron and its environs were given to Caleb to conquer and claim as his inheritance (Joshua 14:12-15). When David was king over Judah, his capital city was Hebron (2 Samuel 5:1-5). Absalom's rebellion began in Hebron (2 Samuel 15:7-12). When the Jews returned to their homeland from captivity in Babylon, some of them preferred to live in Hebron (Kirjath-arba) rather than Jerusalem (Nehemiah 11:25).

heed: to pay careful attention

heir: one who receives the belongings or riches of one who has died

Hell: the place of everlasting torment prepared for the devil and his workers, and for all those who do not receive Jesus Christ as Savior

helmet: a metal covering for the head, worn in battle

help meet (help mate): a suitable helper

heresy (*hair*-uh-see): a denial of something true; untrue statements about God, Jesus, or the church

Hermon: a ridge of mountains about 20 miles long having three peaks, two of them over 9,000 feet and the highest in the land of Palestine. They are located at the southern end of the Anti-Lebanon range, and formed the northern boundary of the Israelite conquest (Deuteronomy 3:8, 9; Joshua 11;3, 17). It has been called Shenir or Senir by the Amorites, Sirion by the Sidonians, and Sion (Deuteronomy 4:48) and Jebel-esh-Sheik, or "Mountain of the Old Man," by the Arabs.

Herod (*hair*-ud): the names of several rulers over Palestine under Roman rule; 1. Herod the Great, ruler of Judea (37-4 B.C.) at the time Jesus was born. At his order the male babies in Bethlehem were killed (Matthew 2:1-18). During his reign the temple in Jerusalem was rebuilt; 2. Herod Antipas, son of Herod the Great, ruled over Galilee and Perea (4 B.C.-A.D. 39). He was responsible for the murder of John the Baptist (Matthew 14:1-12); 3. Herod Agrippa I, grandson of Herod the Great and ruler of Judea (A.D. 37-44). He killed James, the brother of John, with the sword, and imprisoned Peter (Acts 12:1-19); 4. Herod Agrippa II, son of Herod Agrippa I and great-grandson of Herod the Great, was king of the territory east of Galilee (A.D. 48-70). Paul was permitted to plead his cause before him (Acts 25, 26).

Herodians (hair-*ro*-dee-unz): a strong group of influential Jews who supported the Herods and the Roman rule. They joined with the Pharisees in opposing Jesus (Matthew 22:16; Mark 3:6; 12:13).

Herodias (hair-*ro*-dee-us): wife of Herod Antipas, who was the brother of her first husband. John the Baptist condemned Herod for marrying Herodias, and through her influence John was beheaded (Matthew 14:1-12; Mark 6:14-29).

hewer: someone who chops or cuts wood with an ax

Hezekiah (hez-uh-kye-uh): king of Judah for 29 years. Son of Ahaz. Hezekiah was a strong and good king. During his reign, he was influential in destroying false idols, cleansing the temple, and restoring the temple worship. Isaiah, Hosea, and Micah prophesied during the time of Hezekiah (2 Kings 18—20; 2 Chronicles 29—32; Isaiah 36—39; Hosea 1:1; Micah 1:1).

Hiddekel (*hid*-ee-kel): the second major river of Mesopotamia. Hiddekel is the Hebrew name for the Tigris River. It was one of the four rivers flowing from the Garden of Eden (Genesis 2:11-14).

high priest: the head of the priests of Israel; the only one allowed to enter the Most Holy Place

Hilkiah (hil-kye-uh): 1. the high priest in the time of Josiah, king of Judah. He found the lost book of the law while cleaning the temple. He aided the king in a religious reformation (2 Kings 22); 2. father of Jeremiah (Jeremiah 1:1)

hindermost: last

Hinnom, valley of: a valley on the western side of Jerusalem that joins the

Kidron Valley. Human sacrifices were offered here in OT times (2 Kings 23:10). Also called "The Valley of Slaughter" (Jeremiah 19:6).

Hiram (*hye*-rum): king of Tyre during the reigns of David and Solomon. He sent workmen and materials to build a palace for David, and later one for Solomon (2 Samuel 5:11; 1 Kings 5:1-12).

hireling: someone who works for pay

hither: here; near; on this side

Hittites: a tribe of people descending from Ham through his grandson Heth (Genesis 10:15; 1 Chronicles 1:13). They lived in the hill country of Canaan when the Israelites conquered

the land on their return from Egypt (Exodus 3:8; Numbers 13:29).

Hivites: (*hye*-vites): descendants of Ham. One of the groups living in Canaan when the Israelites returned after bondage in Egypt (Exodus 3:8, 17).

holy: 1. pure; perfect; like God; 2. set apart for service to God

Holy Ghost: see **Holy Spirit**

Holy of Holies: see **Most Holy Place**

Holy Place: the front room of the tabernacle (and later the temple), where the table of shewbread, golden candlestick, and altar of incense were kept.

Holy Spirit: a part of the trinity—God the Father, Jesus, and the Holy Spirit. He is the Comforter, sent by Jesus

the high priest

after He ascended back to God. The Holy Spirit directed the writing of the Bible. He lives in each Christian to help him live the Christian life.

honor, honour (*ahn*-er): *n.* respect

honor, honour: *v.* to treat with respect

Hophni (*hahf*-nye): a son of the priest, Eli. The wickedness of him and his brother Phinehas caused a curse to come upon the house of Eli (1 Samuel 2:34; 3:14; 4:11).

Horeb: see **Sinai**

hosanna (ho-*zan*-nuh): a cry or shout of praise; originally a form of prayer that meant, "save now"

Hosea (ho-*zay*-uh): a prophet of Israel who lived during the reign of Jeroboam II. He prophesied in the northern kingdom of Israel when Uzziah, Jotham, Ahaz, and Hezekiah ruled in Judah. He lived and worked at the same time as Isaiah. His book in the OT condemns the unfaithfulness of Israel but stresses God's love and willingness to forgive.

Hoshea (ho-*shee*-uh): son of Elah and the last king of the northern kingdom, Israel. His reign lasted almost nine years, ending with the fall of Samaria (2 Kings 17:1-6).

host: 1. army; a very large number; multitude; 2. a person that receives guests in his home

household: all the people living in the same house

howbeit (how-*bee*-it): although; nevertheless

Huldah: a prophetess during the reign of Josiah. When the scrolls were found in the temple, she identified them as God's law and prophesied the ruin of the nation due to disobedience. Her message influenced reforms carried out by Josiah (2 Chronicles 34:22-28).

humble: modest; lowly; not proud or boastful

Hur: a man of the tribe of Judah who, with Aaron, held up the arms of Moses so that the Israelites could defeat the Amalekites (Exodus 17:10-13)

husbandman: a farmer

hymn (him): a song that gives praise and honor to God

hypocrisy (hip-*ahk*-ruh-see): acting good or religious when one really is not

hypocrite (*hip*-uh-krit): one who pretends to be something that he is not, especially one who pretends to be good or religious when he really is not

hyssop (*hiss*-up): a plant with thick hairy leaves and branches, used by the ancient Hebrews in sprinkling rites

hyssop

Isaiah before God's throne (Isaiah 6)

Ii

I Am: a name for God; the name God himself told Moses

Iconium: (eye-ko-nee-um): an ancient city of Asia Minor. In the time of the NT it was in the Roman province of Galatia, on a road that led to Ephesus and Rome. Iconium was situated on a level plateau about 3,400 feet above sea level, with mountains to the west about 6,000 feet high. Paul and Barnabas brought the gospel to Iconium on Paul's first missionary journey (Acts 13:51—14:7). Paul visited there on his second journey (Acts 18:23). Iconium was possibly one of the cities to whom Paul wrote his epistle to the Galatians.

idol: something that is worshiped as a god, often an image made out of wood, stone, or metal

idolater (eye-doll-uh-ter): one who worships images or objects, such as the sun or moon

Idumea (id-yoo-mee-uh): name used by the Greeks and Romans for the country of Edom (Mark 3:8)

ignorant (ig-nuh-rent): lacking knowledge

ill-favored: ugly

Illyricum (il-lir-ih-kum): a Roman province north of Macedonia on the Adriatic Sea. Paul, in telling of the extent of his ministry, mentions this province (Romans 15:19).

image (im-ij): a picture or figure of something or someone

Immanuel: see **Emmanuel**

immortal: living forever; never dying

immutable (im-myoot-uh-bul): not able to be changed

incarnation (in-kar-*nay*-shun): becoming flesh. Jesus, the Son of God, came to earth and became flesh and blood, but did not give up His divine nature and abilities.

incense: a sweet-smelling substance made of gums and spices to be burned as part of the religious ceremony

infallible (in-*fal*-uh-bul): making no mistakes; unerring

infirmity (in-*fer*-muh-tee): sickness or deformity

inherit: 1. to receive the money or other belongings of someone who has died; 2. to receive from ancestors certain looks or traits—n. **inheritance**

iniquity (in-*ik*-wuh-tee): sin; wickedness

inn: a hotel; a public place to eat and sleep

inspiration (in-sper-*ay*-shun): the special help given by the Holy Spirit to the men who wrote the Bible; literally, "God-breathed"—*adj.* **inspired**

insurrection (in-sur-*rek*-shun): rebellion; a revolt against the government

intercession (in-ter-*sess*-shun): 1. the asking of a favor or making of a request for someone else; 2. a prayer on behalf of another—*v.* **intercede**

Isaac (*eye*-zik): the promised son of Abraham and Sarah. Ishmael was his half-brother (Genesis 21:1-13). While Isaac was still a youth, God told Abraham, as a test of faith, to offer Isaac as a sacrifice. God stopped the hand of Abraham and provided a ram instead (Genesis 22). When Isaac was old and almost blind, his wife Rebekah and his son Jacob tricked him, and he gave the blessing to Jacob rather than his older son, Esau (Genesis 27).

Isaiah (eye-*zay*-uh): the son of Amoz (not the prophet). He lived in Jerusalem. His prophecies mostly concerned Judah and Jerusalem. Because the people were idolatrous and wicked, their nation would be destroyed. A remnant, or small part, however, would be saved. Out of this remnant would be one—the Messiah—who would bring all nations to God. In his book, Isaiah speaks often of the coming of Christ, of His rejection, and of His suffering. Isaiah prophesied during the reigns of four kings of Judah: Uzziah, Jotham, Ahaz, and Hezekiah (2 Kings 19, 20; 2 Chronicles 26:22; 32; book of Isaiah).

Ishmael (*ish*-may-el): son of Abraham and Hagar, Sarah's Egyptian servant (Genesis 16:15, 16). After Isaac his half-brother was born, Ishmael, who was about 16 years old, and his mother were sent away. They made their home in the wilderness of Paran. He became an archer and married an Egyptian woman. He had 12 sons and one daughter (Genesis 21:9-21; 25:12-16; 28:9). His descendants, the Ishmaelites, lived in camps in the desert of northern Arabia. Joseph was sold by his brothers to some Ishmaelites who

Israel (United Kingdom)

Saul (1020-1000)
David (1000-961)
Solomon (961-922)

The Kingdom Divides (922)

Israel (Northern Kingdom)	**Judah** (Southern Kingdom)
Jeroboam (922-901)	Rehoboam (922-915)
	Abijam (915-913)
Nadab (901-900)	Asa (913-873)
Baasha (900-877)	
Elah (877-876)	
Zimri (876)	
Omri (876-869)	Jehoshaphat (873-849)
Ahab (869-850)	
Ahaziah (850-849)	Jehoram (849-842)
Jehoram (849-842)	Ahaziah (842)
Jehu (842-815)	Athaliah (842-837)
	Jehoash (837-800)
Jehoahaz (815-801)	
Jehoash (801-786)	Amaziah (800-783)
Jeroboam II	Azariah (Uzziah)
(786-746)	(783-742)
Zechariah (746-745)	
Shallum (745)	
Menahem (745-738)	Jotham (742-735)
Pekahiah (738-737)	
Pekah (737-732)	Ahaz (735-715)
Hoshea (732-724)	
	Hezekiah (715-687)
Fall of Samaria (722)	
	Manasseh (687-642)
	Amon (642-640)
	Josiah (640-609)
	Jehoahaz (609)
	Jehoiakim (609-598)
	Jehoiachin (598-597)
	Zedekiah (597-587)
	Fall of Jerusalem (587)

Kings of Israel and Judah

were traveling toward Egypt (Genesis 37:25-28).

Israel (*iz*-ray-el): 1. the name God gave to Jacob (Genesis 32:28); 2. Jacob's descendants, the 12 tribes of the Hebrews; 3. the ten tribes that made up the northern kingdom after the time of Solomon; see **Judah**

Israelite (*iz*-ray-el-ite): any descendant of Jacob, whose name God changed to Israel (Genesis 32:28; 35:10); one belonging to the Hebrew people

Issachar (*iss*-uh-kar): ninth son of Jacob, the fifth by Leah (Genesis 35:23). Issachar had four sons. His descendants formed the tribe named for him (Genesis 46:13; Numbers 26:23, 24).

Italy: a boot-shaped peninsula in southern Europe, west of Greece. In the days of the apostles, Italy, as well as most of the civilized world, was ruled from Rome. Cornelius the centurion was of the Italian cohort stationed in Caesarea (Acts 10:1). Aquila and Priscilla lived in Italy for a time (Acts 18:2). Paul's appeal to Caesar involved a journey to Rome and imprisonment there (Acts 27, 28). There were Christians not only in Rome, but in other parts of Italy as well (Acts 28:12-14; Hebrews 13:24).

Ithamar (*ith*-uh-mahr): Aaron's youngest son (Exodus 6:23). After the death of Nadab and Abihu (Leviticus 10:1), Eleazar and Ithamar became priests (Exodus 28:1; 1 Chronicles 24:2-5).

Jj

the fall of
Jericho
(Joshua 6)

Jabbok (*jab*-bahk): an important river east of the Jordan, about 60 miles long. It enters the Jordan about 23 miles north of the Dead Sea and about 43 miles south of the sea of Galilee. Jacob forded the Jabbok River on his way back from Mesopotamia (Genesis 32:22-29).

Jabin (*jay*-bin): 1. a king of Hazor who was defeated by Joshua at the waters of Merom (Joshua 11:1-14); 2. a king of Hazor, probably a descendant of the first one. His commander-in-chief, Sisera, was defeated by Deborah and Barak (Judges 4).

jacinth (*jay*-sinth): a precious stone, orange in color

Jacob: younger twin brother of Esau, son of Isaac and Rebekah (Genesis 25:21-26). He secured the birthright from Esau in exchange for a bowl of stew (Genesis 25:29-34). Jacob and his mother tricked his father into giving him the blessing intended for the firstborn son. The 12 tribes of Israel came from his 12 sons (Genesis 29—37, 42—50).

Jacob's well: a famous well in Samaria, near a town called Sychar

Jael (*jay*-ul): wife of Heber the Kenite. She killed Sisera, captain of Jabin's army, by hammering a tent peg through his head as he slept (Judges 4:17-24).

Jairus (*jay*-ih-rus): a ruler of a synagogue, probably in Capernaum. Jesus raised his little daughter from the dead (Matthew 9:18-26; Mark 5:21-43; Luke 8:40-56).

James: 1. a fisherman, son of Zebedee and brother of John (Mark 1:19). One of the three apostles who were closest to Jesus (Matthew 17:1; Mark 5:37; 14:33). He was beheaded by Herod Agrippa I (Acts 12:2); 2. son of Alpheus, and another apostle of Jesus (Mark 3:18); 3. the brother of Jesus (Matthew 13:55; Galatians 1:19). James did not believe that Jesus was God's Son during His ministry, but after the resurrection he did (John 7:5; 1 Corinthians 15:7). He was a leader in the church in Jerusalem and talked to Paul there (Acts 12:17; 15:13; 21:18; Galatians 1:19; 2:9, 12).

Japheth (*jay*-futh): a son of Noah; brother of Shem and Ham (Genesis 6:10). He and his wife were in the ark during the flood. From him come the Gentile races (Genesis 7:7; 10:2-5).

Jason: a Christian in Thessalonica who invited Paul and Silas to stay in his home while they were visiting the city. Because of this, Jason was dragged from his home and brought before the rulers of the city by the Jews who objected to Paul and Silas. Jason was released only after posting bail (Acts 17:5-9).

jasper: a quartz-like gem, usually green

jealous (*jel*-us): 1. not willing to share someone's love or attention with someone else; 2. hostile toward someone because of something he has; envious; 3. watchful; suspicious

Jebusites (*jeb*-yoo-sites): a tribe of people, descendants of Ham, who were living in the hill country of Canaan before the conquest of the Israelites on their return from Egypt. The Jebusites lived on the site of Jerusalem, which they called Jebus, until the time of David (Joshua 15:8; 2 Samuel 5:6-10).

Jedidah (jeh-*dye*-duh): wife of Amon and mother of Josiah, a good king of Judah (2 Kings 22:1)

Jehoahaz (jeh-ho-uh-haz): 1. son and successor of Jehu. Jehoahaz, a wicked king, ruled Israel in Samaria for 17 years. God allowed enemies to take much of the kingdom from Israel. Just before his death, Jehoahaz prayed to God for help. God restored much of the kingdom after Jehoahaz's death (2 Kings 13:1-9, 22-25); 2. king of Judah, third son of Josiah. He reigned only three months, after his father's death, and then was taken captive to Egypt (2 Kings 23:30-34).

Jehoash: see **Joash**

Jehoiachin (jeh-*hoy*-uh-kin): son and successor of King Jehoiakim of Judah. He ruled three months. King Nebuchadnezzar laid siege to Jerusalem and carried Jehoiachin and his household to Babylon as captives (2 Kings 24:10-15).

Jehoiada (jeh-*hoy*-uh-duh): a high priest in the temple. When the wicked Athaliah killed the royal heirs so she could become queen, Jehoiada's wife, Jehosheba, hid the little boy Joash in the temple. After six years, Jehoiada planned and carried out a revolt against the queen and Joash became king (2 Kings 11; 2 Chronicles 23).

Jehoiakim (jeh-*hoy*-uh-kim): a son of Josiah, king of Judah (2 Kings 23:34, 36). Jehoiakim became king after his brother, Jehoahaz, was carried captive to Egypt. Jehoiakim went back to idol worship. Jeremiah the prophet wrote about the coming punishment of God unless the people repented. Jehoiakim listened to some of the scroll Jeremiah wrote, then he cut it up and burned it (Jeremiah 36). When the Babylonian army besieged Jerusalem, they bound the king to carry him off to Babylon. He died or was murdered, however, before they left the city (2 Chronicles 36:5, 6; Jeremiah 22:18, 19).

Jehoram, Joram (jeh-*hor*-um, *jor*-um): 1. king of Israel, son of Ahab and Jezebel; wicked like his father and mother. He was killed by Jehu (2 Kings 3:1; 9:21-24); 2. king of Judah, the son of Jehoshaphat. He married Athaliah, daughter of Ahab and Jezebel, who influenced him to worship idols. Because of their sin, God sent a terrible plague on the people of Judah, especially on the family of Jehoram. He suffered and died from this disease, and they buried him without mourning (2 Chronicles 21); 3. a priest who taught throughout Judah in the days of Jehoshaphat (2 Chronicles 17:8, 9).

Jehoshaphat (jeh-*hosh*-uh-fat): son and successor of King Asa; one of the good kings of Judah. He destroyed idols and

sent men out to teach the people about God's law. Friendly relations between Judah and Israel came about during his 25-year reign (1 Kings 22:41-50).

Jehosheba, Jehoshabeath (jeh-*hosh*-uh-buh, *jeh*-ho-*shab*-bee-uth): daughter of Jehoram and sister of Ahaziah, both kings of Judah; wife of Jehoiada, the high priest. When Ahaziah was murdered and his mother, the wicked Athaliah, killed the royal heirs, Jehosheba hid the child Joash in the temple until he could be made king (2 Kings 11; 2 Chronicles 22:10-12).

Jehovah (jeh-*ho*-vuh): one of the names of God (Exodus 6:3). Out of reverence, the Jews did not use this name, but instead used "Adonai," which means Lord.

Jehu (*jee*-hyoo): a captain of the army who was later anointed king of Israel. He obeyed God by destroying the house of Ahab and all the worshipers of Baal, but Jehu did not remain faithful in his own worship. His family ruled for 100 years (2 Kings 9, 10).

Jephthah (*jef*-thuh): a God-fearing man, a great captain, he delivered the Israelites from the Ammonites. He was the ninth judge in Israel, and he judged six years (Judges 11:1—12:7).

Jeremiah (jair-uh-*mye*-uh): a great Hebrew prophet of Judah who prophesied during the reigns of Josiah, Jehoahaz, Jehoiakim, Jehoiachin, and Zedekiah. He warned the people that, because of their wickedness, Jerusalem would be destroyed unless they submitted to Babylon. Because of his preaching, he was put in stocks, put in prison, and cast into a dungeon (Jeremiah 20:1-3; 37:1-15; 38:1-6). When Jerusalem was taken, Nebuchadnezzar was kind and gave Jeremiah the choice of going to Babylon or remaining in Jerusalem. Jeremiah chose to stay in the city. Later, Jews fleeing to Egypt compelled him to go with them (Jeremiah 40:1-6; 43:1-7). He was the author of Jeremiah and Lamentations.

Jericho (*jair*-ih-ko): the city of Jericho in the Jordan Valley is considered the oldest city in the world. The OT Jericho was about eight miles northwest of the Dead Sea, and about six miles west of the Jordan. The wall of the city enclosed about seven acres. The city was destroyed by Joshua and the Israelites when they came into Canaan (Joshua 6). It was rebuilt in Ahab's reign by Hiel the Bethelite (1 Kings 16:34). In the NT the road from Jerusalem to Jericho was the scene of the story of the good Samaritan (Luke 10:30-37). Jesus healed two blind men here (Matthew 20:29-34), and it was the home of Zaccheus (Luke 19:1, 2).

Jeroboam (jair-uh-*bo*-um): 1. son of Nebat and Zeruah of the tribe of Ephraim (1 Kings 11:26). Jeroboam was industrious and skillful, and Solomon made him overseer of building operations at Jerusalem (1 Kings 11:28). Ahijah the prophet informed him he would be-

come king of ten tribes. He fled to Egypt, for Solomon sought to kill him (1 Kings 11:29-40). After Solomon's death, he returned. Ten tribes revolted against Rehoboam, Solomon's son, and made Jeroboam their ruler. He set up images of golden calves for the people to worship and led them to sin (1 Kings 12); 2. Jeroboam II was the son of Joash. He ruled over Israel for 41 years. Jonah, Amos, and Hosea prophesied during his reign. Like the first Jeroboam, he led the people to sin greatly (2 Kings 14:23-28; Amos 1:1; 2:6—5:27; Hosea 1—3).

Jerusalem (jeh-*roo*-suh-lem): the sacred city and well-known capital of the united kingdom. It is located about 14 miles west of the Dead Sea and about 33 miles east of the Mediterranean Sea, 2,550 feet above sea level. From Jerusalem, Egypt was about 300 miles southwest, Assyria about 700 miles northeast, Babylon about 700 miles east, Persia about 1,000 miles east, Greece about 800 miles northwest, Rome about 1,500 miles northwest.

David conquered the city and made it his capital (2 Samuel 5:6-10). Solomon built the temple in Jerusalem (1 Kings 6). This was a holy city to the Jews because they came to worship at the temple there. It was the scene of wars and plunderings, and in 586 B.C. the city was destroyed and most of the people were taken captive to Babylon (2 Kings 24, 25). After the Persians had defeated the Babylonians and Cyrus became ruler of Persia, the Jewish exiles were allowed to return to their homeland and rebuild the holy city and the temple (Ezra; Nehemiah).

In Jesus' day Palestine was under Roman rule, but Jerusalem remained the religious center of the Jews. At Passover celebrations and other festivals, Jews would throng to the city from all over the world. Many events in the life of Jesus took place in Jerusalem. Among them are His presentation (Luke 2:22-38), His visit to the temple at age 12 (Luke 2:42-52), and His death, burial, and resurrection (Matthew 26—28; Mark 14—16; Luke 22—24; John 18—20).

The church began in Jerusalem on the Day of Pentecost (Acts 2). Years later the apostle Paul was rescued from a mob and arrested here (Acts 21, 22). Other names used for Jerusalem are: "Zion," "The City of David," "The City of God," and "The Holy City."

Jesse (jess-ee): son of Obed; grandson of Ruth and Boaz (Ruth 4:18-22). He lived in Bethlehem. David was the youngest of his eight sons (1 Samuel 16:10, 11).

Jesus: the name given to our Lord by an angel who visited Mary (Matthew 1:21; Luke 1:31). He was born of a virgin in Bethlehem, spent most of His earthly life in Nazareth, and began His public ministry at the age of 30. He traveled throughout Palestine with His 12 apostles, teaching, performing miracles, and showing the people the will of God. He was falsely accused and crucified on a cross. They

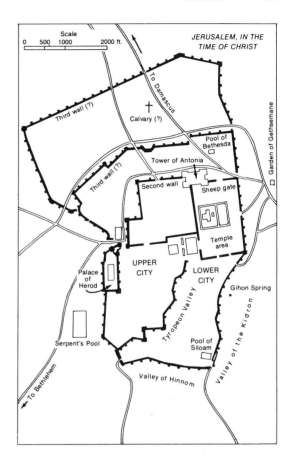

buried Him and sealed the tomb, yet, because He is truly the Son of God, He arose from the dead on the third day. He was seen by many people. Forty days later He ascended into Heaven. He is the Savior of the world. Jesus is in Heaven preparing a place for His faithful followers. He has promised to come to earth again (Matthew, Mark, Luke, and John).

Jethro: a priest in Midian; father-in-law of Moses (Exodus 3:1). During the wanderings in the wilderness, Jethro suggested to Moses that he appoint judges to help him in deciding less important cases among the people. Moses took his good advice (Exodus 18). Jethro is also called Reuel.

Jews: 1. people from the tribe of Judah; 2. all the Hebrews who returned from captivity in Babylon

Jezebel (*jez*-uh-bel): daughter of Ethbaal, king of the Zidonians; wife of Ahab, king of Israel. To please her, Ahab built a temple to Baal (1 Kings 16:30-32). Four hundred and fifty prophets of Baal ate at her table. She threatened Elijah's life, and he had to flee (1 Kings 18, 19). She caused the murder of Naboth (1 Kings 21). She was a wicked queen and died a terrible death (2 Kings 9:7, 30-37).

Jezreel (*jez*-ree-el): a town of Issachar (Joshua 19:18) not far from Mount Gilboa. In ancient times it was at the intersection of trade routes from southern to northern Palestine and to the Jordan Valley. Ahab had a royal palace in Jezreel (1 Kings 18:45, 46). Naboth, who had a vineyard near Ahab's palace, was stoned outside the city (1 Kings 21:1-14). Jezebel met her violent death in Jezreel (2 Kings 9:30-35).

Joab (*jo*-ab): a nephew of David who became commander-in-chief of his army (2 Samuel 2:18; 1 Chronicles 11:4-9). Although he was a brave leader, he was self-centered and ambitious. He killed two men who were his rivals, as well as Absalom, David's son (2 Samuel 3:22-27; 18:9-15; 20:4-10). Joab

was killed in the sacred tabernacle by a man sent from King Solomon (1 Kings 2:28-34).

Joanna: wife of Chuza, Herod's steward. She gave some of her money to Jesus during His ministry. After His death, she went to the tomb with Mary Magdalene and others (Luke 8:3; 24:10).

Joash, Jehoash (*jo*-ash, jeh-*ho*-ash): 1. father of Gideon (Judges 6:11). 2. son of Ahaziah, king of Judah. To usurp the throne, Athaliah, his grandmother, had the brothers of Joash killed while he was still very young. He was saved by an aunt, Jehosheba, who kept him hidden in one of the temple rooms. After six years, Jehoiada, the high priest and husband of Jehosheba, presented the boy Joash to the people, and he was crowned king (2 Kings 11:1-3; 12). At first Joash did well. But after Jehoiada's death, Joash led his people into idol worship. When Zechariah, son of Jehoiada, denounced his sin, Joash had him killed. After a long illness, he was killed in his bed by his servants for the murder of Zechariah. One notable thing accomplished during his reign was the repair of the temple. He ruled for 40 years (2 Chronicles 24; 2 Kings 12).

Job (jobe): a good and devout man who lived in the land of Uz. His faith was tested by some severe troubles. He lost his animals, servants, and his children. He suffered boils all over his body. Job bore all this patiently and did not sin against God. After a time God restored all he had by double measure (book of Job).

Jochebed (*jahk*-uh-bed): a daughter of Levi; wife of Amram; mother of Aaron, Moses, and Miriam (Exodus 6:20; Numbers 26:59)

Joel: 1. oldest son of Samuel. A judge in Beer-sheba, but he took bribes and did evil (1 Samuel 8:1-3); 2. A prophet of Judah who lived during Uzziah's time and wrote a book of the OT

John: a son of Zebedee; brother of James; one of the 12 apostles (Matthew 4:18-22; Mark 3:14-19). He was one of the three closest to Jesus (Matthew 17:1; Mark 5:37; 14:33). He helped Peter prepare the Passover (Luke 22:8), and was present at the trial of Jesus and the crucifixion (John 18:15; 19:26, 27). After the resurrection, he recognized Jesus (John 21:1-7). He was with the group in Jerusalem on the Day of Pentecost (Acts 1:13). He was active with Peter in the early church (Acts 3; 4; 8:14-17), and when very old, was sent to the Isle of Patmos as an exile (Revelation 1:9). John is the writer of five books in the NT: John; 1, 2, and 3 John; and Revelation.

John Mark: see **Mark**

John the Baptist: son of Zechariah the priest and Elisabeth, who lived in the hill country of Judea (Luke 1). John began his ministry in the wilderness of Judea, preaching the baptism of repentance to prepare for the coming of Jesus. He baptized Jesus (Matthew 3). John was imprisoned and put to death by Herod Antipas (Matthew 14:6-12; Mark 6:17-29).

Jonah (*jo*-nuh): the son of Amittai; a prophet from Galilee who lived in the days of Jeroboam II (2 Kings 14:25). God told Jonah to go preach in Nineveh, but he refused and boarded a ship for Tarshish. During a storm he was thrown overboard and swallowed by a great fish. After Jonah prayed for three days and nights he was vomited out on dry land. Jonah then went to Nineveh and preached in that city. The people repented and God spared the city (book of Jonah).

Jonathan (*jahn*-uh-thun): the oldest son of King Saul, and a very close friend of David (1 Samuel 14:49; 18:1-4). He was a brave soldier in his father's army and died in battle at Mount Gilboa (1 Samuel 31:2). Jonathan had a lame son named Mephibosheth, to whom David showed kindness (2 Samuel 9:6, 7).

Joppa: a seaport town of Palestine. The city was built on the rocky heights above the harbor. It was about 35 miles from Jerusalem. Timbers cut in Lebanon were floated from Tyre to Joppa for the building of Solomon's temple (2 Chronicles 2:16) and also for the building of the second temple after the captive Jews returned from Babylon (Ezra 3:7). Jonah boarded a ship at Joppa when he was fleeing from God

(Jonah 1:3). In the NT we find that Peter restored Dorcas to life there (Acts 9:36-43). Peter stayed in Joppa with Simon the tanner, where he received a vision to preach at the house of the Gentile Cornelius (Acts 10).

Jordan: the largest river in Palestine. It rises from sources at the foot of Mount Hermon. In Bible times it flowed through Lake Huleh, the Sea of Galilee, and emptied into the Dead Sea. Including the lakes, and not considering the windings of the river, the Jordan is about 104 miles from Caesarea Philippi to the Dead Sea. Joshua led the Israelites in a miraculous crossing of the river on dry ground (Joshua 3). John the Baptist carried on his ministry near the Jordan (Matthew 3:1-6; Mark 1:4, 5; John 1:28). Jesus was baptized in the Jordan River (Matthew 3:13; Mark 1:9).

Joseph: 1. son of Jacob (Israel) and Rachel. He was the favorite son of his father, and his ten older brothers were jealous. When he was 17, his brothers sold him to some merchants who took him to Egypt. He was sold as a slave but rose to a place of importance second only to Pharaoh. During a severe famine, Joseph's father and brothers came to Egypt for food and were reunited with him (Genesis 37—50); 2. the husband of Mary, who was the mother of Jesus (Matthew 1:16). He was a carpenter (Matthew 13:55), lived in Nazareth (Luke 2:4), and was a descendant of David (Matthew 1:20; Luke 2:4); 3. a Jew of Arimathea and a member of the Sanhedrin. He was a secret disciple of Jesus. With the help of Nicodemus, he buried Jesus in his own new tomb (John 19:38-42).

Joshua: son of Nun, of the tribe of Ephraim (1 Chronicles 7:27); also called Oshea. He was one of the 12 spies sent to explore the land of Canaan (Numbers 13:8, 17), and one of the two who brought back a good report of the land (Numbers 14:6). He became leader of the Israelites at Moses' death. The book of Joshua in the OT tells of the winning of Canaan and the settling of the tribes in the land under Joshua's leadership.

Josiah (jo-sye-uh): king of Judah; son of Amon and Jedidah; grandson of Manasseh. He began to reign when he was eight years old. While repairs were being made to the temple, the lost book of law was found. Josiah had it read publicly, and its teachings were used as the basis for a great religious reformation. Josiah, the last good king of Judah, reigned 31 years and died in battle (2 Kings 22:1—23:30; 2 Chronicles 34, 35). Jeremiah and Zephaniah prophesied during the latter years of Josiah's reign (2 Chronicles 35:25; Jeremiah 1:1, 2; Zephaniah 1:1).

jubilee year: a celebration that the people of Israel held every fifty years, in which all land was to revert back to its original owner

Judah (joo-duh): 1. the fourth son of Jacob; son of Leah. He persuaded his brothers not to kill Joseph, but rather to sell him to some merchants (Genesis 37:26); 2. the name of the tribe descended from Judah; 3. the kingdom of Judah, which began when the ten northern tribes, called Israel, rebelled and withdrew from King Rehoboam (1 Kings 12—22). The kingdom was in the southern part of the country and consisted of the remaining tribes of Judah and Benjamin.

Judas (*joo*-dus): 1. Judas, or Jude, a brother of our Lord (Matthew 13:55). Other brothers listed are James, Joses, and Simon. He is thought to be the author of the book of Jude in the NT: 2. Judas (not Iscariot), one of the 12 apostles (Luke 6:16; John 14:22). He is also called Thaddeus (Matthew 10:3; Mark 3:18); 3. Judas Iscariot, son of Simon (John 6:71). He was one of the 12 apostles (Mark 3:19) and was made their treasurer (John 12:6; 13:29). He betrayed the Lord for 30 pieces of silver and then went out and hung himself (Matthew 27:1-10; Acts 1:18); 4. Judas, who lived in Damascus, in a street called Strait. Saul stayed with Judas at the time of his own conversion (Acts 9:11); 5. Judas of Galilee who, in the days of the enrollment, raised a revolt (Acts 5:37; Luke 2:2); 6. Judas, whose surname was Barsabas. He was a leader in the church at Jerusalem (Acts 15:22-32).

Jude: writer of the last epistle in the NT. A brother of the Lord (Jude 1; Matthew 13:55; Mark 6:3); see **Judas** (1)

Judea, Judaea (joo-*dee*-uh): most of the exiles who returned from Babylon belonged to the tribe of Judah. Their land came to be called Judea (Ezra 5:8). It was a small province south of Samaria, much like the earlier kingdom of Judah. In the time of Jesus, Judea was one of the three provinces west of the Jordan: Galilee on the north, Samaria in the central area, and Judea to the south (see map, p. 91). Judea was made a part of the Roman province of Syria. It was governed by an officer appointed by the Roman emperor and was subject to the governor of Syria.

judge: 1. a public official who hears and decides cases in a court of law; 2. a person chosen by God to be a military ruler of the Israelites before the nation had kings. There were twelve of these judges; 3. a title for God or Christ

judgment: 1. a decision given by someone in authority; 2. some great trouble supposed to be sent by God; 3. the final judging of all people by God

judgment seat: the chair on which a judge (1) sat while holding court

Julius (*jool*-yus): a Roman centurion responsible for taking Paul and other prisoners from Caesarea to Rome. He showed kindness to Paul and saved his life at the time of the shipwreck (Acts 27).

justification (jus-tih-fih-*kay*-shun): the act or process of being made right—v. **justify**

Moses at Kadesh-barnea (Numbers 20)

Kk

Kadesh, Kadesh-Barnea (kay-desh—bar-nee-uh): a place about 50 miles south of Beersheba, in the northeastern part of the Sinai peninsula. It was on the border between the Wilderness of Paran and the Wilderness of Zin (Numbers 13:3, 26; 20:1; 27:14). Kadesh was the headquarters of the Israelites for much of the time they wandered in the wilderness. Moses sent spies from there to Palestine (Numbers 13:21-26; 33:37, 38; Deuteronomy 1:46; 2:14). Miriam died and was buried at Kadesh (Numbers 20:1). There Moses disobeyed God by striking the rock for water rather than speaking to it (Numbers 20:2-13).

Kedesh (kee-desh): a town northwest of Lake Huleh where the tribe of Naphtali settled. It was the home of Barak. Deborah and Barak gathered the armies of Israel there to fight against Sisera and the army of Jabin (Judges 4:4-10).

Keturah (keh-tyoo-ruh): the second wife of Abraham, who bore him six sons who became ancestors of Arabian tribes (Genesis 25:1-6; 1 Chronicles 1:32, 33). This marriage probably took place after the death of Sarah and the marriage of Isaac (Genesis 24:67—25:1).

Kidron (kid-run): a deep valley, or ravine, east of Jerusalem. It separates the city and the Mount of Olives, then continues southeast to the Dead Sea. In Bible times the spring of Gihon supplied water for a brook to flow in the valley. This brook was diverted into a tunnel to the Pool of Siloam as a source of water for the city during Hezekiah's reign (2 Chronicles 32:3, 4). Jesus passed over the Kidron whenever He went from Jerusalem to the Garden of Gethsemane (John 18:1). This valley was a familiar sight to all who were in Jerusalem.

kindred: relatives

kine: cattle

kingdom: the country or area ruled by a king

kingdom of God (of Heaven): all those on earth and in Heaven who love God and obey Him

kinsman: a relative

Kish: a man of the tribe of Benjamin; father of King Saul (1 Samuel 9:1, 2)

Kishon: (kye-shahn, kish-ahn): a river of central Palestine, which flows northwest through the valley of Jezreel (Esdraelon) and on to the Mediterranean Sea. In the dry summer season the river flows only in its last seven miles, where it receives water from springs at the base of Mount Carmel. Barak and Deborah led the Israelites to victory against the army of Sisera along this river (Judges 5:19-21). On the southern bank of the river the prophets of Baal were destroyed after the contest with Elijah on Mount Carmel (1 Kings 18:40).

Kittim: see **Cyprus**

knit: to draw together or grow together

Kohath (ko-hath): second son of Levi, ancestor of Moses and Aaron (Exodus 6:16-20). His descendants, one of three divisions of the Levites, cared for the furniture of the tabernacle (Numbers 4:1-15).

Korah (ko-rah): 1. son of Esau (Genesis 36:14); 2. a Levite, descendant of Kohath. He and two others went against Moses and Aaron. For disobeying, they and their followers were swallowed up by an earthquake (Numbers 16); 3. a Levite from whom came the Korahites, doorkeepers and musicians in the tabernacle and the temple. His sons are named in the titles of some Psalms.

Lazarus (John 11)

Laban (*lay*-bun): son of Bethuel and grandson of Nahor, who was Abraham's brother. Laban lived in Padanaram (Genesis 24:15; 28:5). He was the brother of Rebekah and allowed her to go to Canaan and become Isaac's wife (Genesis 24).When Jacob fled from Esau, he went to Laban. He served Laban 14 years to receive his daughters, Leah and Rachel, in marriage (Genesis 27:41—31:55).

Lachish (*lay*-kish): a royal city of Canaan and later a Judean border fortress, 25 miles southwest of Jerusalem. Inhabited as early as 3000 B.C. One of the last cities of Judah to fall to the Babylonians, around 587 B.C. (Jeremiah 34:7)

Lamb of God: lambs were offered as sacrifices to God under the law; this became a name for Jesus because He was offered on the cross as a sacrifice for sin

lame: crippled or disabled

Lamech (*lay*-muk): 1. a descendant of Cain. He had three sons; one invented musical instruments, one invented metalcraft, and the third founded the nomadic life (Genesis 4:17-22); 2. son of Methuselah and father of Noah (Genesis 5:25-31)

lamentation (lam-en-*tay*-shun): sorrow shown by loud crying or weeping

lamp: the ordinary lamp was made of baked clay. At first, lamps were like saucers to hold the olive oil, with a pinched lip to hold the wick. Later the lamp had a

lamp

cover and closed tube, something like a short teapot spout, for the wick. Sometimes lamps were made in one piece with a hole in the top where the oil was poured in. The wick was placed in a short spout on one side.

Laodicea (lay-*ahd*-ih-*see*-uh): a wealthy city in Asia Minor; a leading banking center. Famous for its glossy black wool and for its medical school; mentioned by John in Revelation 3:14-22.

Lappidoth (*lap*-ih-doth): husband of Deborah, who was a judge in Israel (Judges 4:4)

lasciviousness (las-*siv*-ee-us-ness): having desires that are wrong; lustfulness

Lasea (luh-*see*-uh): a seaport on the southern side of the island of Crete. It was about five miles east of the bay of Fair Havens. The ship taking Paul to Rome passed by Lasea (Acts 27:8).

latchet: a small leather strap that held a sandal on the foot

laver (*lay*-ver): a large brass basin with water, placed between the altar of burnt offering and the door of the tabernacle. It was used by priests to wash their hands and feet before serving in the tabernacle.

laver

law: 1. rules of conduct given by a person in authority; 2. the Ten Commandments and the rest of the rules God gave Moses; 3. the first five books of the OT

lawyer: one who was trained in the Jewish law and taught it to others; see **scribe**

Lazarus (*laz*-uh-rus): 1. brother of Mary and Martha. Their home was in Bethany. Jesus raised Lazarus from the dead (John 11); 2. the beggar in the parable of the rich man and Lazarus (Luke 16:19-31)

Leah (*lee*-uh): the older daughter of Laban; sister of Rachel. She became the first wife of Jacob. She was the mother of Reuben, Simeon, Levi, Judah, Issachar, Zebulun, and Dinah (Genesis 29:20-35; 30:17-21).

learned (*ler*-ned): having much knowledge

leaven (*lev*-en): 1. a form of yeast used to make bread rise; 2. something that causes change; 3. influence; teachings

Lebanon (*leb*-uh-nun): high mountain range, extending for 100 miles along the Syrian coast of the Mediterranean Sea. The mountains were famous for their great cedar trees, used by Solomon in building the temple and palace at Jerusalem (1 Kings 5, 7).

leek: a garden herb

legion (*lee*-jun): 1. a huge number; 2. a division of 6,000 soldiers, the largest single unit in the Roman army

lentils: bean-like vegetables, often dried and ground into meal

leper: a person having a severe skin disease called leprosy; because it was contagious, a leper was not allowed to live with other people. He had to live outside the walls of the city and cry "unclean!" to warn people to stay away from him

leprosy (*lep*-ruh-see): a severe disease of the skin

Levi (*lee*-vye): 1. Jacob's third son; his mother was Leah (Genesis 35:23). He was born in Haran and accompanied his father on his return to Canaan. He joined his brothers in the plot against Joseph (Genesis 37); 2. another name for Matthew (Matthew 9:9-13; Mark 2:14-17; Luke 5:27-32)

Levites (*lee*-vites): the descendants of Levi, the son of Jacob. The men of this tribe were to care for the tabernacle (Numbers 1:50-53). The priests were Levites belonging only to the family of Aaron (Exodus 28:1). Levites received no tribal land, but 48 cities were given to them (Numbers 35:1-8). They were supported by tithes (Numbers 18:21-24).

libation (lye-*bay*-shun): a liquid offering, such as olive oil, poured on an altar; a drink-offering

Libertines (*lib*-er-teenz): probably Jews who had been prisoners of Roman generals and were later given their freedom. They had a synagogue in Jerusalem and were enemies of Stephen (Acts 6:9).

Libya: the ancient Greek name for northern Africa west of Egypt. Cyrene was one of its principal cities. Jews from Libya were in Jerusalem on the Day of Pentecost (Acts 2:10). Simon, who carried Jesus' cross, was from Cyrene of Libya (Matthew 27:32).

lineage (*lin*-ee-ij): a group of people descended from a common ancestor; the other relatives descended from this ancestor

lintel

lintel (*lin*-tul): the crosspiece over the top of a door

lo: "Look!"

locust: a kind of grasshopper

Lois: Timothy's grandmother, a woman of great faith (2 Timothy 1:5)

longsuffering: patience; long and patient endurance of an offense or trouble

loom: a frame used in weaving cloth

lord: 1. owner; 2. master; one who has power and authority

Lord's Day: the first day of the week; the day Jesus came forth from the grave; Sunday

Lord's Supper: the eating and drinking of bread and grape juice to remember the death of Jesus Christ. The unleavened bread represents His body and the "fruit of the vine," or grape juice, represents His blood that

Lord's Supper

was shed for the forgiveness of our sins. This remembrance, which Jesus began the night before He died, was held each Lord's Day by the NT church.

Lot: son of Haran; nephew of Abraham; grandson of Terah. He went to Canaan with Abraham (Genesis 11:31; 12:5). He settled near Sodom (Genesis 13:11, 12), and later was rescued from the city (Genesis 19:1-29).

lots: objects, thrown on the ground or drawn from the hand, used to determine what the will of God is

Lucas: see **Luke**

lucre (*loo*-ker): money; profit

Luke: a physician and a close companion of the apostle Paul (Colossians 4:14; Philemon 24). He was a Gentile Christian, probably from Antioch of Syria. He traveled with Paul on some of his missionary journeys (Acts 16:10-17; 20:5—21:16). He was with Paul in Rome (2 Timothy 4:11). Luke was also an accurate historian and wrote the Gospel of Luke and the book of Acts, both in the NT. His Gospel gives many events in the life of Christ not recorded in the other Gospels.

lust: a strong desire for some kind of pleasure or need, often referring to sexual desire

Lycaonia (*lik*-ay-*oh*-nee-uh): a high, rugged inland district of southern Asia Minor. The land was good for grazing sheep and cattle. The people spoke a strange dialect. At the time of the apostle Paul, the region, except for a very small area in the extreme east, was a part of the Roman province of Galatia. Three of its cities were Lystra, Derbe, and Iconium. Paul preached in some cities of Lycaonia (Acts 14).

Lycia (*lish*-ee-uh): a province of Asia Minor, jutting south into the Mediterranean Sea. Paul, on his last voyage to Jerusalem, landed at Patara, one of the port cities of Lycia (Acts 21:1, 2). On Paul's voyage to Rome he changed ships at Myra, another seaport of Lycia (Acts 27:5, 6).

Lydda (*lid*-uh): a town about 30 miles northwest of Jerusalem and about 11 miles southeast of Joppa. Its OT name was Lod (Nehemiah 11:35). At Lydda Peter healed Aeneas, a man with palsy, and the miracle led many to believe in the Lord (Acts 9:32-35).

Lydia: a woman of Thyatira, who lived in Philippi. She made her living by selling costly purple dyes or dyed goods. When Paul arrived in Philippi, she accepted Jesus gladly and became the first convert in Macedonia and Europe. Paul and his companions stayed in her home for a time. Later, when Paul and Silas were released from prison, they returned to her home (Acts 16:14-40).

lyre (*lye*-ur): a musical instrument some-thing like a harp

lyre

Lystra (*liss*-truh): a city of Lycaonia in the Roman province of Galatia, about 18 miles southwest of Iconium. When Paul healed a crippled man here, people tried to worship Paul and Barnabas as gods (Acts 14:6-21). Paul visited Lystra again later (Acts 16:1-5 18:23). He first met Timothy at Lystra or Derbe (Acts 16:1).

shipwreck at Melita (Acts 27)

Mm

Macedonia (*mass*-ih-*do*-nee-uh): in NT times Macedonia was a Roman province, directly north of Greece, and at the northwest corner of the Aegean Sea. Paul was called to preach in Macedonia by a vision from God (Acts 16:9-12). After Paul left, Timothy and Silas continued the work there (Acts 17:14). Later Paul visited again in the region (Acts 20:1-3; 2 Corinthians 2:13; 7:5; 1 Timothy 1:3).

Macedonians (*mass*-uh-*do*-nee-unz): people who lived in Macedonia

Machpelah (mak-*pee*-luh): a place near Hebron where there was a field with trees and a cave. Abraham purchased this place from Ephron, a Hittite, for 400 shekels of silver, to be used as a burial place for Sarah (Genesis 23). Abraham, Isaac, Rebekah, Jacob, and Leah were also buried here (Genesis 49:29-33; 50:12, 13).

Magdala (*mag*-duh-luh): a town on the western shore of the Sea of Galilee, three miles north of Tiberias; the home of Mary Magdalene (Luke 8:2).

Magdalen, Magdalene (*mag*-duh-len, *mag*-duh-leen): see **Mary** (3)

magistrate (*maj*-uh-strait): a government official who sees that the laws are carried out

magnify: to praise highly

Mahlon (*mah*-lahn): the older son of Elimelech and Naomi, and the first husband of Ruth (Ruth 1:2; 4:10)

majesty (*maj*-uh-stee): royal power and dignity

Malachi (*mal*-uh-kye): a prophet, and the author of the last book of the OT. He prophesied during the time of Nehemiah.

Malchus (*mal*-kus): a servant of the high priest at the time of Jesus' arrest. Peter cut off his ear and Jesus healed it (Luke 22:50, 51; John 18:10).

malefactor (*mal*-uh-fak-ter): one who does something against the law

malice (*mal*-iss): ill will; the desire or wish for pain, injury, or trouble to happen to another

Malta: see **Melita**

mammon: money; worldly riches or possessions

Mamre (*mam*-ree): a place about two miles north of Hebron where oak trees grew. Abraham lived there (Genesis 13:18; 14:13). At Mamre Abraham was visited by three heavenly messengers (Genesis 18:1-16). Abraham bought a field east of Mamre in Machpelah as a burial place for Sarah (Genesis 23). Isaac spent his last years in Mamre (Genesis 35:27).

Manaen (*man*-uh-en): a Christian teacher or prophet in the church at Antioch when Paul and Barnabas were set apart as missionaries to the Gentiles. He was the foster brother of Herod Antipas (Acts 13:1-4).

Manasseh (muh-*nass*-uh): 1. the older son of Joseph and brother of Ephraim (Genesis 41:50, 51). One of the tribes of Israel was descended from Manasseh (Numbers 1:34, 35); 2. a wicked king of Judah, son of good king Hezekiah (2 Kings 21)

mandrake: a narcotic plant, the roots of which were thought to help a woman to conceive a child; also called "love apple"

manger: a box in a stable to hold feed for cattle and horses

manifest (*man*-uh-fest): *v.* to make evident or easily seen; to display

manifest: *adj.* easily seen or understood

manifold: many; varied

manna: a food God provided for the Israelites as they wandered in the wilderness after leaving Egypt. The food fell from Heaven and looked like frost upon the ground, and went away when the sun shone on it. The Israelites were told to gather only as much as they would eat each day, except on the sixth day, when they were to gather enough for the Sabbath. If they took too much manna, the extra spoiled. It could be ground and made into bread, and was sweet-tasting.

manner: 1. kind; sort; 2. style; fashion; 3. the way someone acts; behavior; 4. way; method

Manoah (muh-*no*-uh): the father of Samson; a Danite from the town of Zorah (Judges 13:2; 16:31)

mantle: a large, loose outer garment without sleeves

mantle

Marah (*may*-ruh): a place in the wilderness of Shur where the Israelites found bitter water three days after they crossed the Red Sea. God told Moses to throw a certain tree into the water, and the water was made sweet (Exodus 15:22-25).

Marcus: a Roman name for Mark; see **Mark**

Mark: his first name was John (Acts 12:12). The home of his mother, Mary, in Jerusalem, was one of the meeting places of Christians (Acts 12:12-17). He went along with Paul and Barnabas on their first missionary journey to Cyprus, but he left them at Perga, for some unknown reason, and returned to Jerusalem (Acts 12:25; 13:5, 13). Paul refused to take Mark on his next journey. Barnabas took Mark and returned to Cyprus (Acts 15:36-41). Later, Paul recommended Mark to the church in Colosse (Colossians 4:10). Mark was with Paul in Rome (Philemon 24). Mark wrote a record of the life of Jesus, the Gospel of Mark.

marketplace: an open place in a street or town where people bought and sold

Mars' Hill: see **Areopagus**

Martha: the sister of Mary and Lazarus, and a close friend of Jesus. He was a guest in their home in Bethany (Luke 10:38-42; John 11).

martyr (*mar*-ter): one who is persecuted or killed because of his beliefs

marvel (*mar*-vul): n. something wonderful or amazing

marvel: v. to feel wonder or amazement

Mary: 1. the mother of Jesus (Matthew 1, 2; Luke 1, 2). A cousin of Elisabeth and a descendant of David (Luke 1:36; Acts 2:29, 30; Romans 1:3; 2 Timothy 2:8). She was present at the first miracle performed by Jesus in Cana (John 2:1-11), and later was concerned for

His safety (Matthew 12:46; Mark 3:21, 31). Mary was at the cross and in the upper room after Jesus' ascension (John 19:25-27; Acts 1:14); 2. Mary of Bethany, sister of Martha and Lazarus. She anointed the feet of Jesus (John 11:2; 12:3); 3. Mary Magdalene. She lived in Magdala. Jesus cast seven devils out of her (Mark 16:9; Luke 8:2), and she became one of His most devoted followers. She was at the cross and burial of Jesus (Matthew 27:56-61). Early the third day, following Jesus' death, she came with other women to the tomb. Jesus appeared first to her (Mark 16:1, 2, 9); 4. mother of James and Joses. She was present at the crucifixion and came to the tomb early the third day after (Matthew 27:56—28:1); 5. Mary, mother of John Mark, a Christian in Jerusalem. Her home was often used as a meeting place of Christians. Peter went there right after his release from prison (Acts 12:1-17).

Massah (*mass*-uh): one of the names given by Moses to the place where he struck a rock to draw water for the grumbling Israelites on the way to Sinai (Exodus 17:1-7). The other name given was Meribah.

master: a name given to Jesus, meaning "Teacher"

Matthew: a Jew, living in Capernaum, who collected Roman taxes from the people (Matthew 9:1, 9). Jesus called Matthew to follow Him, and he did. He had a great feast in his home in honor of Jesus. Matthew is also called Levi (Luke 5:27-32). Matthew is the author of the Gospel of Matthew in the NT.

Matthias (muh-*thy*-us): the follower of Jesus who was chosen to fill the place of Judas as one of the twelve apostles (Acts 1:21-26)

measure: *n.* a container made to hold an exact amount

Medes (meeds): people who lived in the land of Media, an ancient powerful

a marketplace

empire of Asia (2 Kings 17:6; Esther 1:19)

mediator (*mee*-dee-ay-ter): one who acts to bring about agreement between two or more persons

meditate: to pray; to think about someone or something quietly and intensely

meek: humble; gentle—*n.* **meekness**

Megiddo (muh-*gid*-oh): an important city in north central Palestine. It was situated on the south side of the Plain of Esdraelon. It was strategically located at the entrance to a pass across the Carmel mountain range and on the main highway between Asia and Africa. Militarily it served as a key to the defense of the Jordan Valley and the coastal plain. Megiddo was conquered by Joshua (Joshua 12:21). It was fortified by Solomon and was one of his garrison cities for horses and chariots (1 Kings 9:15-19). Ahaziah, king of Judah, died there (2 Kings 9:27), and King Josiah lost his life in battle with Pharaoh-necho at Megiddo (2 Kings 23:29; 2 Chronicles 35:22-24).

Melita (*mel*-ih-tah): an island in the Mediterranean Sea, about 60 miles south of Sicily. It is now called Malta. Paul and his companions stayed there three months when their ship was wrecked on the way to Rome (Acts 27, 28).

memorial (muh-*mor*-ee-ul): something (like a monument, speech, or ceremony) that helps one remember a person or event

Mephibosheth (muh-*fib*-oh-sheth): the son of Jonathan; grandson of King Saul. When he was five years old, he was crippled in an accident (2 Samuel 4:4). After Jonathan's death, David showed kindness to him (2 Samuel 9:6-13).

merchant: a person who buys and sells

mercy: more kindness and goodness than one deserves or expects

Meribah (mer-ih-bah): see Massah

Meshach (mee-shak): the Babylonian name given to Mishael, one of the princes of Judah, when they were taken captive by Nebuchadnezzar. He and two of his friends refused to bow down to the king's image. With the help of God, they escaped death in the fiery furnace (Daniel 1:7; 3:13-30).

Mesopotamia (mess-o-po-*tay*-mee-uh): the region between the Tigris and Euphrates Rivers, extending from the Persian Gulf to the mountains of Armenia. In the Hebrew the region is called Aram, Aram-naharaim, or Padan-aram. Some of the cities of Mesopotamia were Haran, Nahor, and Pethor (Genesis 11:31; 24:10; Deuteronomy 23:4). In the NT the term covered all the territory of Babylonia and Sumer, as well as Ur of the Chaldees (Acts 7:2), and Syria.

Messiah (muh-*sye*-uh): "The Anointed One." The word "messiah" was originally used for any person who had been anointed with holy oil, as the high priest or the king (Leviticus 4:3, 5, 16; 2 Samuel 1:14, 16). But the title came to have a greater meaning. It referred to the coming promised Savior and Deliverer for whom the people waited (Jeremiah 23:5, 6; Isaiah 9:6, 7; Micah 5:2-5).

mete: to measure

Methuselah (muh-*thoo*-zuh-luh): the son of Enoch, and the oldest man who ever lived. He was 969 years old when he died (Genesis 5:26, 27).

Micah: a prophet to both Israel and Judah, who prophesied during the reigns of Jotham, Ahaz, and Hezekiah. The book he wrote is found in the OT.

Michmash (*mik*-mash): a village in the section of land inhabited by the tribe of Benjamin. It was eight miles northeast of Jerusalem. Several notable battles took place here (1 Samuel 13, 14; Isaiah 10:28; 37:36). Michmash was a fair-sized town at the time of the return of the captives from Babylon (Ezra 2:27).

Midian: an area in the northern part of the Arabian Desert beyond the Jordan, in eastern Edom and Moab, and in the eastern part of the Sinai Peninsula. After Moses killed an Egyptian, he fled to Midian (Exodus 2:11-15).

Moses' father-in-law was a priest in Midian (Exodus 3:1).

Midian: a son of Abraham and Keturah (Genesis 25:1-6)

Midianites (*mid*-ee-un-ites): descendants of Midian. Although the Midianites were nomads, they had great wealth in the time of Moses. In the time of the judges, they entered Canaan and took the crops of all who had sown them. Gideon led the Israelite army to victory against them (Judges 6—8).

midst: middle; a position of being among or surrounded by others

midwife: a woman hired to assist at the birth of a child

mile: a unit of length; the Jews used the Roman mile, which was a little less than our mile

Miletus (mye-*lee*-tus): a seaport city about 36 miles south of Ephesus. Paul waited at Miletus for a meeting with the elders from Ephesus (Acts 20:15-38). Later he returned there and left Trophimus, who was ill (2 Timothy 4:20).

mill: two heavy stones, one on top of the other, which were used to grind grain into flour

millstone

millet: a kind of grain

Millo: a mound or rampart built up by filling with stones and earth; 1. an ancient fort in or near Shechem. Judges 9:6, 20 no doubt refers to the people who lived in the tower or fortification; 2. a place outside Jerusalem David built up (2 Samuel 5:7-9). Solomon later strengthened Millo (1 Kings 9:15, 24; 11:27). Three hundred years later Hezekiah again strengthened Millo (2 Chronicles 32:5). King Joash was killed here by his servants (2 Kings 12:20, 21).

minister: one who serves others

minstrel: someone who played a musical instrument; minstrels played in the courts of kings and at funerals

miracle: (mir-uh-kul): a special act of God not done by natural means; in the Bible called "signs," "wonders," or "mighty acts"

mire: soft mud, often quite deep

Miriam: the daughter of Amram and Jochebed; sister of Moses and Aaron (Exodus 15:20; Numbers 26:59). When just a girl, she helped protect her baby brother until the princess of Egypt found him (Exodus 2:3-9). After the Israelites left Egypt and crossed the Red Sea, Miriam led the women in singing praises to God. Because she complained about Moses' foreign wife, she was stricken with leprosy, but was healed after Moses prayed for her. She died at Kadesh before entering the promised land (Exodus 15:20, 21; Numbers 12; 20:1).

mite: small coin worth less than a penny

Moab (mo-ab): Moab was a rolling plateau of rich pasturelands lying east of the Dead Sea. On the east was the Arabian Desert, and Edom was to the south.

Moabites (mo-uh-bites): descendants of Moab, son of Lot, who was a nephew of Abraham. They lived east of the Dead Sea (Genesis 19:30-38; Exodus 15:15). The Moabites refused the Israelites permission to pass through their land (Judges 11:17). They were defeated by David (2 Samuel 8:2, 12; 1 Chronicles 18:2, 11) and denounced by the prophets (Isaiah 15; 16; 25:10; Jeremiah 9:25, 26; 48; Ezekiel 25:8-11). Ruth, daughter-in-law of Naomi, was a Moabitess (Ruth 1:4).

mock: to ridicule or make fun of someone

molten: 1. made by melting and casting; 2. melted; 3. glowing

moneychanger: a kind of banker who sat in the temple. Since only the shekel could be given as an offering to God, these men took foreign money and gave shekels in return.

Moriah (mo-rye-uh): a place about 50 miles from Beersheba, where Abraham prepared to offer his son Isaac as a sacrifice (Genesis 22:1-14). Mount Moriah was also the place where Solomon built the temple in Jerusalem (2 Chronicles 3:1).

Moses: son of Amram and Jochebed, of the tribe of Levi. His brother was Aaron and his sister was Miriam. He was born in Egypt. When Pharaoh ordered all male babies killed, Moses' mother placed him in a basket on the Nile River. The princess found him and reared him as her son (Exodus 2:1-10). When Moses was grown, he became involved in the murder of an Egyptian. Moses fled to Midian, where he kept the flocks of Jethro, and married Zipporah, a daughter of Jethro (Exodus 2:11-25). God called Moses to lead the Israelites out of Egypt (Exodus 3:1-10). On Mount Sinai, God gave him the Ten Commandments on two tablets of stone (Exodus 19, 20, 32—34). Moses led the people during their years in the wilderness. With God's guidance, he organized Israel with civil and religious laws. When the people finally came to the entrance of the promised land, Moses gave his farewell address, then climbed to the top of mount Nebo, where he viewed the promised land and died (Exodus, Leviticus, Numbers, Deuteronomy). Moses was a great leader. He wrote the first five books of the OT.

mote: a small speck of dust or dirt

Mount of Olives: a ridge of four hills running in a north-south direction east of Jerusalem. They are separated from the city by the Kidron Valley. Usually the term refers to the two center hills that are directly across from the temple area. These two center hills have a dip between, and an elevation of almost 2,800 feet. The garden of Gethsemane was near or at the foot of the mount on the west side. David went up the Mount of Olives when he fled from Absalom (2 Samuel 15:30). Jesus' triumphal entry into Jerusalem began on the Mount of Olives (Matthew 21:1). On its slope He wept over Jerusalem (Luke 19:37-41). Jesus was praying in Gethsemane when He was arrested (Matthew 26:30). From this mount He ascended back to Heaven (Acts 1:9-12).

mourn: to weep or cry because someone has died or because of some other sad occasion. Sometimes mourners were paid to cry loudly at funerals—n. **mourner**

multitude: a very large number of people; a crowd

murmur: to grumble; to complain in a low tone of voice

Myra: a city of Lycia, in Asia Minor, where Paul was transferred to a grain ship from Alexandria when he was a prisoner on his way to Rome (Acts 27:5, 6). In Paul's day, this port was an important stop for Egyptian grain ships that sometimes sailed directly to Myra before July 20, when the westerly winds changed to northwesterly.

myrrh (mur): a reddish-brown spicy-smelling gum made from the bark of trees growing in Arabia. It is used for anointing, for perfuming, to deaden pain, and to prepare bodies for burial.

myrrh

myrtle tree: a small evergreen, the wood of which was valuable

Mysia (mish-ee-uh): a province in the northwest part of Asia Minor. It was mountainous and had thick forests. It included such cities as Troas, Assos, and Pergamum. Paul and Silas traveled through the area on Paul's second missionary journey (Acts 16:7, 8).

King Nebuchadnezzar (Daniel 4)

Nn

Naaman (nay-uh-mun): the commander of the army of Ben-hadad, king of Syria. He was a leper, and was healed by the prophet Elisha (2 Kings 5).

Naboth (nay-bahth): owner of a vineyard in Jezreel. He refused to sell it to King Ahab, and Queen Jezebel had him falsely accused and put to death. As Ahab was about to take over the vineyard, the prophet Elijah met him and foretold his doom (1 Kings 21).

Nadab (nay-dab): the oldest of Aaron's four sons. A priest of the tabernacle (Exodus 28:1). He and his brother Abihu made a strange offering to the Lord, and God killed them with fire (Leviticus 10:1-7).

Nahor (nay-hor): son of Terah; brother of Abraham; father of Bethuel (Genesis 24:15). The name is sometimes spelled Nachor (Joshua 24:2).

Nahor (nay-hor): The city of Nahor was considered to be Haran, but it may have been a settlement a little below

Haran, perhaps founded by Nahor (Genesis 24:10).

Nahum: (*nay*-hum): an OT prophet of Judah, probably while Josiah was king. He spoke of the doom of Nineveh.

Nain: a town about six miles southeast of Nazareth. There Jesus stopped a funeral procession and restored a widow's son to life (Luke 7:11-17).

Naomi (nay-*oh*-mee): wife of Elimelech. Her husband and two sons died while they were living in Moab. She returned to Bethlehem with her daughter-in-law, Ruth (Ruth 1—4).

Naphtali (*naff*-tuh-lye): 1. the sixth son of Jacob, the second by Bilhah (Genesis 35:25): 2. one of the 12 tribes, which descended from Naphtali (Numbers 26:48-50)

Nathan (*nay*-thun): a prophet during the reigns of David and Solomon. David consulted him regarding the building of the temple (2 Samuel 7; 1 Chronicles 17). Later he rebuked David for his great sin with Uriah and Bathsheba (2 Samuel 12). He helped in the development of the temple music (2 Chronicles 29:25), and wrote a history of the reign of David (1 Chronicles 29:29) and at least part of the reign of Solomon (2 Chronicles 9:29).

Nathanael (nuh-*than*-yel): see **Bartholomew**

naught, nought: nothing

Nazarene (naz-ur-*een*): one who lived in Nazareth; Jesus was sometimes called by this name

Nazareth: a town in a secluded valley in lower Galilee, north of the plain of Esdraelon. It was about 15 miles southwest of Tiberias. It was the home of Mary and Joseph (Luke 1:26, 27). Jesus grew to manhood in Nazareth and lived there until He was about 30 years of age (Luke 2:39-52; 3:23). He taught in the synagogue of the city (Luke 4:16).

Nazarite: a man or woman who made a promise to do some special service for God, and was set apart to do that service. A Nazarite was not to drink wine, cut his hair, or come in contact with a dead body.

Neapolis: (nee-*ap*-oh-lus): the seaport of Philippi, situated about ten miles east of the city on a neck of land between two bays of the Aegean Sea. Paul landed here when he came from Troas obeying his call to Macedonia (Acts 16:11, 12).

Nebo: a mountain of the Abarim range in Moab across from Jericho. It was on Mount Nebo, from the summit of Pisgah, that Moses looked over into Canaan. He died without entering the promised land (Numbers 27:12; Deuteronomy 34).

Nebuchadnezzar (*neb*-yoo-kud-nez-er): a powerful king of Babylon. He attacked Jerusalem three times and took captives to Babylon. Among these were Daniel and his noble friends (Daniel 1—4). In 586 B.C. Nebuchadnezzar destroyed Jerusalem, including the beautiful temple, and took the outstanding people of Judah captive (2 Kings 24; 25; 2 Chronicles 36:5-21; Jeremiah 52:12-15). Sometimes spelled *Nebuchadrezzar.*

Nebuzaradan (*neb*-yoo-zar-*ay*-dun): a general in Nebuchadnezzar's army when the Babylonians took Jerusalem (Jeremiah 52:12-30)

Negeb, Negev: (*neg*-ub, *neg*-uv): the dry area south of Judea beginning a few miles south of Hebron and extending to Kadesh-barnea. It is about 4,500 square miles of desert. Beersheba is an oasis in the north Negeb. The Negeb is called "the South" in several passages of Scripture.

Nehemiah (*nee*-uh-*mye*-uh): son of Hachaliah. He was a Jew in exile and a cupbearer to Artaxerxes, king of Persia (Nehemiah 2:1). He received permission from the king to lead a band of captives back to Jerusalem to rebuild the wall of the city. He was a man of great courage and ability. He organized the community, and the wall was rebuilt in 52 days (Nehemiah 2:11—6:15). Nehemiah worked with Ezra to instruct the people in God's law (Nehemiah 8).

Nicodemus (*nik*-uh-*dee*-mus): a leading Pharisee and member of the Sanhedrin. He came at night to talk to Jesus (John 3:1-21). He mildly defended Jesus at the feast of Tabernacles (John 7:40-53). After the death of Jesus, Nicodemus and Joseph of Arimathea came boldly with rich spices for embalming Jesus' body and helping with the burial (John 19:38-42).

nigh: near

Nile: the main river of Egypt and Africa. It is one of the few rivers that run from south to north. Beginning at Lake Victoria, it flows over 4,000 miles to empty into the Mediterranean Sea, making it the longest river in the world. Between Khartoum and Aswan the river goes through six cataracts. They are numbered from north to south in the order of their discovery. This great river provided the Egyptians with drinking water, fish for food, washing and bath facilities, and water for irrigation. Much of northeast Africa would not be livable without the Nile. Several Bible references to the Nile are found in the latter part of Genesis and the early chapters of Exodus. Baby Moses was placed on the Nile in a basket of bulrushes (Exodus 2:3-5). In one of the plagues the Nile turned to blood (Exodus 7:20, 21).

Nimrod: great-grandson of Noah, through Ham. He was a mighty hunter before the Lord and a powerful leader. He began such great cities as Babel and Nineveh (Genesis 10:8-12).

Nineveh (*nin*-uh-vuh): the capital city of the ancient Assyrian Empire. Nineveh

Noah (Genesis 6—8)

was founded by Nimrod shortly after the flood. The city was located on the east bank of the Tigris River, about 300 miles north of Babylon. It was protected by five walls and three moats, and had an estimated population of more than 600,000. Nineveh rose to world power in about 900 B.C. The Assyrians were a wicked, mighty, warring, and brutal people. In about 785 B.C. God sent Jonah as a missionary to Nineveh, telling them to repent and turn aside from their brutal conquests. Many repented, and God spared the city for a time (book of Jonah). By 721 B.C. the Assyrian armies had destroyed the northern kingdom of Israel. The prophet Nahum foretold the overthrow of Nineveh (book of Nahum). This prophecy was fulfilled in about 612 B.C. when the Babylonians besieged the city for two years and completely destroyed it.

Noah: son of Lamech and grandson of Methuselah. He was a righteous man. Because of the wickedness of other people, God decided to destroy them. He told Noah to build an ark according to His plans. Noah was to take his wife, his sons, Shem, Ham, and Japheth, their wives, and male and female of all living creatures into the ark. After the flood waters went down, the ark rested on Mount Ararat. Noah built an altar and offered sacrifices to God. God put a rainbow in the sky as a token of His promise never again to destroy the world with a flood (Genesis 5:28—9:29).

nobleman: 1. royalty; 2. one from a wealthy, important family

Nod: a place east of Eden where Cain went after he had killed his brother Abel (Genesis 4:16)

nomad (no-mad): one who wanders from place to place

nought, naught: nothing

nourish (nur-ish): 1. to nurture; to help something grow; 2. to feed

Nun: of the tribe of Ephraim and father of Joshua (Numbers 13:8)

nurture: v. to take care of something or someone and help it to grow

nurture: n. training; upbringing

a poor woman's offering (Mark 12)

Oo

oasis (o-*ay*-sis): a place in the desert where water and trees are found

oath: a serious promise, often made calling upon God as witness

Obadiah (oh-buh-*dye*-uh): 1. the governor of King Ahab's palace. During the persecution by Queen Jezebel, he hid 100 prophets of God in a cave. While the country was suffering from a drought, Elijah sent Obadiah to announce his presence to King Ahab. Elijah's interview with Ahab led to the contest on Mount Carmel (1 Kings 18); 2. a prophet of Judah, author of a short book in the OT that tells of the destruction of the Edomites, descendants of Esau

Obed (*oh*-bed): son of Boaz and Ruth; grandfather of David (Ruth 4:13-17)

obeisance (oh-*baiss*-enss): a deep bow; an act of humility or submission

oblation (oh-*blay*-shun): something offered in worship or devotion; an animal sacrifice

offend: to insult; to sin against God

offering: something given as part of worship. In the OT God told the Israelites to give animals, crops, wine, or oil as sacrifices. Today the money we give God can also be called an offering.

ointment: a very expensive salve made of oil and perfume

omega (oh-*may*-guh): 1. the last letter of the Greek alphabet; 2. last; ending

omer (*oh*-mur): a unit of measure for dry capacity. Its exact amount is not known, but it contained from two to three-and-one half quarts.

omnipotent (ahm-*nip*-oh-tent): almighty; all-powerful—*n.* **omnipotence**

omniscient (ahm-*nish*-ent): all-wise; all-knowing—*n.* **omniscience**

Omri (*ahm*-ree): sixth king of Israel, a good soldier but a bad king; father of Ahab (1 Kings 16:21-28)

Onesimus (oh-*nes*-ih-mus): a runaway slave of Philemon in Colossae. Paul converted him in Rome and sent him back to Philemon, requesting Philemon to receive him back as a brother in Christ (book of Philemon). Onesimus and Tychicus carried the letter to Philemon and one to the Christians at Colossae.

onyx (*ahn*-iks): a precious stone that has layers of different shades of color

Ophrah (*ahf*-ruh): a town west of the Jordan in the territory of Manasseh, probably at the south edge of the plain of Esdraelon, at the foot of Mount Gilboa. It was the home of Gideon, one of the judges, where God commanded him to deliver Israel from the Midianites (Judges 6:11-24).

oppress (uh-*press*): to use power and authority to crush or burden people

oracles (*or*-uh-kuls): the words of God

ordain: 1. to set someone apart for a special office or duty; 2. to decree; to establish a law or an order

ordinance (*or*-dih-nunss): a law given by someone in authority; an order

Orpah: wife of Chilion and daughter-in-law of Naomi. She chose to stay in Moab rather than return to Bethlehem with Naomi and Ruth, her sister-in-law (Ruth 1:4-14).

Oshea: see **Joshua**

Othniel (*ahth*-nee-el): the son of Kenaz. He won the daughter of Caleb in marriage by capturing the city of Debir. He became a judge over Israel, and delivered the Israelites from the oppression of the king of Mesopotamia. The land then had rest for forty years (Judges 1:11-13; 3:7-11).

an oasis

Christ before Pilate (John 19)

Pp

Padan-aram (*pay*-dun—*ay*-rum): a region in upper Mesopotamia. Abram and his family lived in its chief city, Haran, before going to Canaan. Abraham sent a servant to Padan-aram to get a wife for Isaac (Genesis 25:20). Jacob fled to Padan-aram from Esau (Genesis 28:2, 5). It is also called Mesopotamia, Aram, and Aram-naharaim ("Aram between the rivers").

Palestine: the word "Palestine" originally came from "Philistia," the land of the Philistines. This was the land west of the Jordan River. This country was first called Canaan (Genesis 12:5). Later, Palestine referred to the land east and west of the Jordan. This land was about 70 miles wide and 150 miles long, from the mountains of Lebanon on the north to Beersheba in the south. Its east and west boundaries were the Arabian Desert and the Mediterranean Sea. Before the conquest led

by Joshua, the land was inhabited by Canaanites, Hittites, Horites, Amorites, and Amalekites. Under the leadership of Moses, the Israelites conquered the region east of the Jordan River, and later under Joshua, the people crossed the Jordan River. After many battles they conquered the region west of the Jordan. From that time on, the history of Palestine is largely the history of the Israelites.

In NT times, the area of Palestine east of the Jordan was divided into Decapolis and Perea. West of the Jordan, Palestine was divided into Galilee, Samaria, and Judea. At that time the country was ruled by Rome. (See map, p. 91)

palsy (*pahl*-zee): a disease of the nerves, sometimes causing shaking or a withering of the hand

Pamphylia (pam-*fill*-ee-uh): a province of southern Asia Minor, bounded on the south by a gulf of the Mediterranean, on the north by Pisidia, on the east by Cilicia, and on the west by Lycia. It consisted of a plain about 80 miles long and about 25 miles wide. There were some Jews living there, and some of them were present in Jerusalem on the Day of Pentecost (Acts 2:10). The apostle Paul visited there (Acts 13:13; 14:24; 15:38).

Paphos (*pay*-fahs): the capital city of Cyprus, a large island in the Mediterranean Sea. In Paphos Paul confronted a magician, and it led to the conversion of the Roman governor of the island (Acts 13:6-13).

parable: a short story that teaches a lesson

paradise (*pair*-uh-dise): a part of Hades; where the dead go to await Heaven

Paran (*pay*-run): a wilderness region somewhere in the very southern part of Palestine, including Kadesh-barnea. Most scholars think it was in the northeast part of the Sinai Peninsula. Ishmael lived in Paran (Genesis 21:21). After the Israelites left Mount Sinai, they camped in this area (Numbers 10:12; 12:16). Moses sent out spies from Paran to search out the land of Canaan (Numbers 13:3, 26). It is also referred to as El-Paran (Genesis 14:6).

parchment: the skin of a goat or sheep, prepared so that it can be used to write on

Parthians (*pahr*-thee-unz): a people who occupied a region some distance southeast of the Caspian Sea, called Parthia. The area today is known as a part of Iran. Parthians were present in Jerusalem on the Day of Pentecost (Acts 2:9).

Passover: 1. the "passing over" of the homes of the Israelites when the first-born sons of all the Egyptian families were killed (Exodus 12); 2. a week-long feast of the Jews, held each year to remind the people of the first "passing over" (see chart, p. 44)

pastor: shepherd, bishop; elder

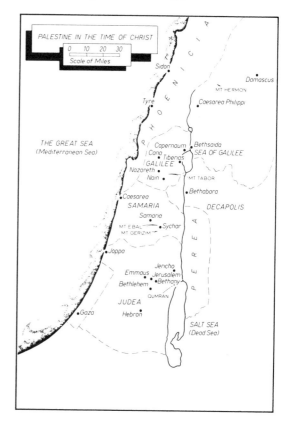

patriarch (*pay*-tree-ark): 1. a father or ruler of a family or tribe; 2. a founder of the Hebrew nation

Paul: a Jew named Saul of the tribe of Benjamin; a Pharisee, yet a Roman citizen (Acts 21:39; Philippians 3:5). He was born in Tarsus, a chief city in Cilicia. He was educated in the law by the well-known Gamaliel, and also learned the trade of tentmaking (Acts 18:3; 22:3). Saul became a strong leader in Judaism and he actively opposed and persecuted Christians. He was a witness to the stoning of Stephen (Acts 7:58—8:3). As he was traveling to Damascus to persecute more Christians, an event changed the course of his life. In a vision he heard the voice of Jesus. Saul knew then that Jesus truly lives and is the Son of God. Saul became a Christian and a great apostle to the Gentiles (Acts 9:1-20). As the apostle Paul, he made three missionary journeys establishing churches in Asia Minor, Macedonia, and Greece. He suffered much for his faith. During his imprisonment in Rome, he wrote some of the epistles. The following books in the NT were written by Paul: Romans, 1 and 2 Corinthians, Galatians, Ephesians, Philippians, Colossians, 1 and 2 Thessalonians, 1 and 2 Timothy, Titus, Philemon, and probably Hebrews. His life and works are recorded by Luke, his close companion, in the book of Acts, chapters 7:58—8:3; 9:1-31; 11:22-30; 12:24, 25; 13—28.

pence: pennies

penitent (pen-ih-tent): sorry for one's sins and willing to stop doing wrong

Paul and Silas in prison (Acts 16)

penny: a Roman coin also called a *denarius*

Pentateuch (*pen*-tuh-tyook): the first five books of the OT

Pentecost (*pent*-ih-kost): the Greek name for the Jewish Feast of Weeks, held fifty days after the Passover feast

penury (*pen*-yuh-ree): poverty

peradventure: perhaps; possibly

perdition (per-*dih*-shun): Hell; damnation

perfect (*per*-fekt): *adj.* without fault or defect; having nothing wrong; mature

perfect (per-*fekt*): *v.* to improve or refine; 2. to remove all faults; 3. to rid of sin and uncleanness

Perga: the chief city of old Pamphylia in Asia Minor. It is located about 12 miles inland from its seaport of Attalia. A famous temple of Diana was in the vicinity. Paul and Barnabas visited the city during their missionary travels (Acts 13:13, 14; 14:24, 25).

perilous (*pair*-uh-lus): dangerous

perish (*pair*-ish): to die; to become ruined

Perizzites (*pair*-ih-zites): an important tribe of the Canaanite people, sometimes mentioned as one of the tribes of Palestine. They were in the country as early as the days of Abraham (Genesis 15:20; Exodus 3:8; Joshua 11:3).

perplexed: puzzled; confused

persecute (*per*-sih-kyoot): to injure or harm someone because of his beliefs; to inflict suffering on another—*n.* **persecution**

persevere (per-suh-*veer*): to endure; to continue on in spite of trouble or discouragement—*n.* **perseverance**

Persia: Persia was a country on a mountainous plateau east of the lower end of the Tigris-Euphrates valley. It became a world power, and its great empire was so large it reached from India on the east to Greece on the west. Its capitals were Persepolis and Susa, and sometimes Babylon. Cyrus founded the empire by defeating Media and Babylon in 539 B.C. Cyrus the Great permitted the Jews exiled in Babylon to return to their homeland (2 Chronicles 36:22, 23; Ezra 1). Darius I, another great Persian ruler, allowed the Jews to rebuild their temple in Jerusalem (Ezra 6). In 486 B.C. Xerxes I came to the throne. He was probably the "Ahasuerus" referred to in Ezra 4:6 and in the book of Esther. During the reign of Darius III (335-331 B.C.) the Persians were defeated by the armies of Alexander the Great of Greece.

Persians: people who lived in Persia. When Babylon was defeated by Cyrus, king of Persia, Palestine came under Persian rule.

perverse: 1. turned away from and opposed to what is right and good; 2. wicked; corrupt

pestilence: a disease that spreads rapidly and causes many deaths

Peter: the name Jesus gave to Simon (John 1:40-42; Matthew 16:18), a brother of Andrew. Both were fishermen on the Sea of Galilee when Jesus called them to be His followers (Matthew 4:18-20). Peter was one of Jesus' favored three apostles—Peter, James, and John—and was privileged to be with Jesus at His transfiguration (Matthew 17:1, 2), the raising of Jairus' daughter (Mark 5:37-42), and the agony in the garden (Matthew 26:36, 37). Peter was an outstanding leader in the early days of the church, as recorded in the first few chapters of Acts. Acts 2 records his great sermon delivered on the Day of Pentecost. Two books in the NT, 1 and 2 Peter, were written by the apostle Peter.

petition: to ask; to make a request

Pharaoh (*fay*-ro): a title used for the kings of Egypt

Pharisees (*fair*-uh-seez): a strong Jewish religious group in NT times. They were trained in the OT law and added many strict rules of their own. They believed in the resurrection of the dead and in life after death. They were very much against Jesus because He was not the kind of political Messiah they wanted.

Phenice, Phoenix (fih-*nye*-see, *fee*-niks): a harbor on the southern coast of Crete. The grain ship from Alexandria on which Paul was traveling to Rome tried to reach this harbor during a severe storm (Acts 27:12).

Philemon (fye-*lee*-mun): a Christian in Colossae. His runaway slave was converted by Paul in Rome. Paul wrote to Philemon and asked him to forgive Onesimus and to receive him back as a brother in Christ.

Philip: 1. one of the 12 apostles. He lived in Bethsaida. He brought Nathanael to Jesus (John 1:43-49). Philip was present at the feeding of the 5,000 (John 6:5, 6). After the resurrection and ascension he was with the group in the upper room in Jerusalem (Acts 1:13); 2. one of the seven deacons chosen by the early church (Acts 6:5). Persecution scattered the Christians, and Philip became an evangelist. He preached in Samaria, performed miracles, and won people to Jesus, including Simon the sorcerer and the Ethiopian eunuch (Acts 8).

Philippi (fih-*lip*-pye): a city in northeast Macedonia, situated about ten miles northwest of its seaport, Neapolis. A mountain range separated the two cities, but they were connected by the great Egnatian Road that ran from Rome to Asia. Paul and Silas visited Philippi and made converts, including Lydia and the Philippian jailer (Acts 16:11-40). The church at Philippi was the first one established in Europe. This church was generous and sent gifts to Paul (Philippians 4:14-17; 2 Corinthians 11:9). His letter to the Philippians in the NT was written in part to acknowledge their gifts.

Philistia (fih-*liss*-tee-uh): the land of the Philistines. It was the plain of Canaan that lay between Joppa and Gaza, an area about 50 miles long and about 15 miles wide.

Philistines (fih-*liss*-teenz): an ancient warlike people who inhabited the area along the Mediterranean Sea. The Philistines caused the Israelites much trouble during OT times. Palestine derived its name from the Philistines.

Phinehas (*fin*-ee-us): 1. son of Eleazar and grandson of Aaron (Exodus 6:25). He was a high priest who is known for his fight against the idol worship of the Moabites (Numbers 25); 2. an unworthy son of the high priest, Eli. He and his brother, Hophni, because of their wickedness, caused a curse to come on the house of Eli (1 Samuel 2:34; 3:14; 4:11).

Phoenicia (fuh-*nish*-ee-uh): an ancient country along the Mediterranean coast with the Lebanon mountains on the east. It extended from Arvad on the north to Mount Carmel on the south, a distance of about 125 miles. The chief cities were Tyre and Sidon. The territory had good natural harbors, and the mountains on the east afforded the Phoenicians a great supply of timber from which ships were constructed.

The Phoenicians became the most skillful navigators in the world. They not only traded with different countries, but established colonies in areas that were favorable for commerce.

Jesus visited the coasts of Tyre and Sidon (Matthew 15:21; Mark 7:24, 31). Paul came to this area on his third missionary journey (Acts 21:1-3).

Phrygia (*frij*-ee-uh): In Paul's day most of Phrygia was in the province of Asia, but a small part of it was in the province of Galatia. Jews from Phrygia were present in Jerusalem on the Day of Pentecost (Acts 2:10). The apostle Paul evangelized in this region on his missionary tours (Acts 16:6; 18:23).

phylactery (fuh-*lak*-ter-ee): a small leather box, containing some of the OT law, that Jewish men tied to their arms or foreheads at the time of prayer

phylactery

piety (*pye*-uh-tee): showing religious respect; reverence

Pilate (*pye*-lut): a Roman governor of Judea (Luke 3:1). Jesus was brought before him to be tried, and Pilate in his cowardly weakness delivered Jesus to be crucified (Matthew 27:1-26; Luke 23:1-24; John 18:28—19:22).

pilgrimage (*pill*-grum-ij): a trip to a sacred place

ships of Phoenicia

pillar: 1. a large post, often decorated, that supports a building; 2. a person or thing that greatly supports something else

pillar of cloud, pillar of fire: a miraculous cloud in the form of a pillar that led the Israelites by day on their way from Egypt to the promised land. God showed His presence in the pillar of cloud; at night, the Israelites were led by a pillar of fire.

pipe: a musical instrument something like a flute

Pisidia (pih-*sid*-ee-uh): a district in Asia Minor, about 120 miles east to west, and 50 miles north to south. It was bounded on the east by Lycaonia, on the west by Caria, on the north by Phrygia, and on the south by Pamphylia and Lycia. The area was filled with ranges of the Taurus Mountains with many wild mountaineers and bandits. In about 25 B.C. the Roman ruler Augustus began subduing them by establishing a chain of Roman posts, which included Antioch and Lystra on the north side. Pisidia was still very dangerous when Paul and Barnabas traveled in the area (Acts 13:14; 14:24).

Pison, Pishon (pye-sun, pye-shun): one of the four rivers that flowed from Eden (Genesis 2:11)

pitch: a black, sticky material used to seal something against water and make it watertight

plague (plaig): *n.* 1. a disaster, thought to be sent as a punishment from God; 2. a dangerous contagious disease that spreads rapidly and often causes death

plague: *v.* to annoy or aggravate someone; to cause someone worry or distress

plowshare: the part of the plow that goes into the ground and turns the soil

pollute: 1. to destroy the pureness or cleanness of anything; 2. to make something dirty

Pontus: an ancient district of Asia Minor along the Black Sea. Jews from this province were in Jerusalem on the Day of Pentecost (Acts 2:9). A Jewish Christian named Aquila was born in Pontus (Acts 18:2). Peter addressed his first letter to Jewish Christians in Pontus (1 Peter 1:1).

potentate (*po*-tun-tait): one who has controlling power

Potiphar (*pah*-tih-fer): the captain of Pharaoh's guard and owner of Joseph. His wife influenced Potiphar to imprison Joseph on a false charge (Genesis 39:1-20).

pottage (*paht*-ij): a thick soup made with herbs and lentils, and sometimes with meat

praise: to glorify, compliment, or commend

pray: 1. to ask something; 2. to talk to God

precept: a rule; a principle

presbytery (*prez*-bih-tair-ee): a group of elders

prey (pray): 1. an animal that is hunted and killed for food; 2. one who is helpless or unable to resist attack; a victim

pride: the state of being pleased with oneself, especially because of something he possesses or something he has done; conceit

priest (preest): a man from the tribe of Levi who served God by offering sacrifices, teaching the law, and taking care of the tabernacle or temple. Moses, at God's direction, appointed Aaron to be the first priest, soon after the Israelites had left Egypt, and after God had given Moses the law.

principality (prin-sih-*pal*-uh-tee): 1. the office or authority of a prince; 2. the territory ruled by a prince

Priscilla: wife of a Jewish Christian named Aquila. They were tentmakers Paul met in Corinth (Acts 18:2). Priscilla and Aquila helped Paul in telling others about Jesus. They instructed Apollos in Ephesus (Acts 18:24-26), where a church met in their home (1 Corinthians 16:19). Paul sent them greetings in Rome (Romans 16:3).

privily (*priv*-uh-lee): secretly; privately

proclaim: to declare publicly; preach— n. **proclamation**

proconsul (pro-*kahn*-sul): a Roman official who served as a deputy consul to help govern a province, usually for a one-year term

procurator (*prahk*-yer-ay-ter): the governor of a Roman province appointed by the emperor

prodigal (*prah*-dig-ul): n. one who spends foolishly

prodigal: *adj.* wasteful

profane: *v.* to treat something sacred with abuse or contempt

profane: *adj.* not holy; not concerned with religion

profession (pro-*fesh*-un): 1. a statement of one's beliefs or opinions; 2. a career or vocation

prophecy (*prahf*-uh-see): 1. a statement of the will of God; 2. something told or written that will happen in the future

prophesy (*prahf*-uh-sye): 1. to speak in behalf of God; 2. to teach about religious matters; 3. to predict future happenings

prophet (*prahf*-et): 1. one who spoke God's message to the people; 2. one who told events that would happen in the future; 3. a man who spoke in another's place

propitiation (pro-*pish*-ee-*ay*-shun): an act or gift that regains someone else's good will or favor

proselyte (*prah*-suh-lite): 1. a stranger or foreigner; 2. a Gentile who had accepted the Jewish religion

prosper: to succeed at something; to become strong

proverb: a brief, wise saying

providence (*prahv*-uh-denss): God's guidance and care of the universe

province (*prahv*-inss): a division of an empire, such as Rome, that was ruled by an official

provoke: to annoy or aggravate someone; to make someone angry—*n.* **provocation**

prudent (*prood*-ent): having good judgment in one's actions; wise; discreet

pruninghook: a large pole with a sharp blade on one end, used for cutting off branches

psalm (sahlm): a song or poem used in worship

psaltery (*sahl*-tuh-ree): a musical instrument used in worship, thought to be like a zither or autoharp with ten strings

publican: a man who collected taxes for the Roman government

psaltery

Publius (*pub*-lih-us): the chief person on the island of Melita. He gave food and lodging to Paul and his companions after their shipwreck on the rocky shore (Acts 27:39—28:11).

pulse: vegetables with seeds that can be eaten, such as peas, beans, or lentils

pure: 1. clean; uncontaminated; 2. free from sin or guilt

pulse

purge: 1. to clear of guilt; 2. to cleanse and make free of impurities

purification (pyoor-if-ih-*kay*-shun): ceremonial cleansing that was required by the Jewish law at four times: (1) after the birth of a child; (2) after contact with a dead body; (3) after certain diseases; (4) after having a running sore. Purification was done by washing in water and by offering sacrifices.

Puteoli (pyoo-*tee*-oh-lye); an important seaport in Italy on the Bay of Naples, where the ship carrying Paul and other prisoners to Rome landed. Because Puteoli was a trading center, many Jews lived there. Paul enjoyed the hospitality of Christians there before on to Rome (Acts 28:13, 14).

quail is sent to the Israelites (Numbers 11)

quail: a small brown bird that lives in fields and is used for food

quaternion (kwah-*tur*-nee-un): a four-man Roman guard

quicken: to make alive

Quirinius: (kwih-*rin*-ee-us): see **Cyrenius**

quit: to conduct oneself in a certain way

Rahab hides the spies (Joshua 2)

Rr

rabbi (rab-eye): a title meaning "teacher" or "master"

raca (*rak*-uh): an insulting word meaning "empty" or "worthless"

Rachel: younger daughter of Laban. She was the favorite wife of Jacob and the mother of Joseph and Benjamin (Genesis 29:9-30; 30:22-24; 35:16-19).

Rahab (*ray*-hab): a woman whose house was on the wall of the city of Jericho. She hid the two spies whom Joshua sent to explore the city. Later when the city was captured, she and her family were saved because of her kindness to the spies (Joshua 2:1-22; 6:17-25). She was an ancestress of David, and thus in the family of the Christ (Matthew 1:5).

raiment: clothing

ram: a male sheep

Ramah (*ray*-muh): 1. Ramah in Benjamin, a town located on a hill about five miles north of Jerusalem, was the headquarters of Deborah, a judge of Israel (Judges 4:5); 2. Ramathaim-zophim (ray-muth-*ay*-um-*zo*-fum) was a town set in the hill country of Ephraim. It was the birthplace of Samuel (1 Samuel 1:1, 19, 20; 2:11), the headquarters of his judicial circuit (1 Samuel 7:17; 8:4; 15:34), and his burial place (1 Samuel 25:1, 28:3).

ram's horn: a trumpet made from the horn of a ram, used to call people together for worship or soldiers to battle

ransom: *v.* to rescue; to deliver from captivity by paying a price; 2. to free from sin

ransom: *n.* the price paid to free a slave or captive

raven: a large black bird

reap: to harvest grain

reason (ree-zun): *n.* a cause or explanation

reason: *v.* 1. to think; 2. to discuss

Rebekah: daughter of Bethuel and sister of Laban. When Abraham sent his servant to Nahor in Mesopotamia to choose a wife for his son, Isaac, Rebekah was chosen. She and Isaac had twin sons, Jacob and Esau (Genesis 24; 25:19-34).

rebel (ree-*bel*): *v.* to disobey or oppose the law, God, or those in authority

rebel (*reb*-ul): *n.* someone who disobeys or opposes the law, God, or those in authority

rebuke: 1. to reprimand or criticize strongly; 2. to restrain; to turn back

Rechabites (ree-kuh-bites): a Kenite tribe who lived among the Israelites. Their chief was Jonadab, son of Rechab. He commanded his people to live a simple life, drink no wine or intoxicating drink, plant no vineyards, and build no houses, but rather live in tents (Jeremiah 35).

reckon (*rek*-un): 1. to count or estimate; 2. to consider; to think about something

reconcile (*rek*-un-sile): to resolve; to bring someone back into friendship or harmony—*n.* **reconciliation**

redeem: 1. to buy back or win back; 2. to set free; rescue—*n.* **redemption**

Redeemer: one who saves others; a name for Jesus

reed: 1. a unit of length equal to about eleven feet; 2. a tall grass that grows near streams

refiner: one who heats metal, especially gold or silver, to clean it

refuge, cities of: six cities set aside by Moses as places of safety for anyone who accidentally killed someone. Here the accused could stay until a fair trial could be held.

regeneration (ree-*jen*-er-*ay*-shun): the act of restoring to original condition; being born again

Rehoboam (ree-huh-*bo*-um): son of King Solomon and Naamah, a wife who was of the Ammonites. When Rehoboam became king, the people of the 12 tribes begged him to lower the heavy taxes that Solomon had placed on them. Rehoboam refused, and ten tribes revolted and made Jeroboam their king (1 Kings 11:26—12:24; 2 Chronicles 10—12). The nation was never again united. Rehoboam ruled in Judah 17 years, and his son, Abijam, became king (1 Kings 14:21, 31).

reign (rain): *v.* to rule

reign: *n.* the period of time in which a certain ruler is in power

reins (rainz): the kidneys; used figuratively to mean the center of the emotions (much as we use the word "heart")

rejoice: to be glad or happy

remission (ree-*mish*-un): the act of being released from guilt and sin, or from illness

remnant: 1. a small amount or number remaining from the original group; 2. a small part left over

rend: to tear; to tear the hair or clothing as a sign of anger, grief, or despair—*past tense,* **rent**

repent: to change one's own heart, mind, and direction; to be sorry for sin and decide to turn to God—*n.* **repentance**

Rephidim (*ref*-ih-dim): the last place where the Israelites camped before they reached Mount Sinai. Here the people complained against Moses because they had no water to drink. The place was then called Meribah and Massah (Exodus 17:1-7). At Rephidim Joshua defeated the Amalekites while Aaron and Hur held up the hands of Moses (Exodus 17:8-16).

replenish (ree-*plen*-ish): to fill with persons or animals

reproach: *v.* to blame; to express disappointment or disapproval

reproach: *n.* blame

reprobate (rep-ro-bait): worthless; condemned

reprove (ree-*proov*): to correct; to criticize with the intent to help someone

requite (ree-*kwite*): 1. to pay back; 2. to do harm in return for something

rereward (reer-ward): *n.* a rear guard

respecter: a giver of special attention to some persons over others

restitution (res-tih-*too*-shun): the act of restoring something to its original condition; making good for some injury

resurrection (rez-uh-rek-shun): coming to life again after dying

Reuben: oldest son of Jacob (Genesis 29:32). When his brothers plotted to kill Joseph, he persuaded them to throw him into a pit instead (Genesis 37:17-36). Reuben was the founder of one of the 12 tribes of Israel.

Reuel (*roo*-el): see Jethro

reveal (ree-*veel*): to uncover something; to make something known

revelation (rev-uh-*lay*-shun): the making known or revealing of God's will; unveiling

revellings (*rev*-uh-lingz): wild parties

reverence: honor; devotion; respect; see **piety**

revile (ree-*vile*): to use abusive language toward someone; to persecute with name-calling or untrue words

Rhegium (ree-jih-um): a town on the southern tip of Italy, across from Messina in Sicily. The ship carrying Paul stopped here on his voyage to Rome (Acts 28:13).

Rhoda: a servant girl of Mary, the mother of John Mark (Acts 12:12-17)

Rhodes (rohdz): a large island southwest of Asia Minor, lying near Crete in the Mediterranean Sea. Its capital city had the same name. In its harbor once stood one of the seven wonders of the world, the Colossus of Rhodes. It was a bronze statue of a sun-god, about 105 feet high, holding a javelin in one hand and a torch in the other. This huge statue straddled the opening through which ships came into the harbor. The ship in which Paul sailed from Assos to Jerusalem stopped at Rhodes (Acts 21:1).

righteous (rye-chuss): *adj.* 1. right and good; 2. free from guilt or sin; without fault—*n.* **righteousness**

righteous: *n.* people who do right

rod: a wooden club used by shepherds to protect their sheep from wild animals

Rome: a city in west central Italy, on the western bank of the Tiber River, founded in 753 B.C. After an early period of constant warfare Rome became a republic, and later the capital of a world empire. It was during the time of the Great Roman Empire that Jesus was born and the events recorded in the NT took place.

Ruth: a Moabite woman, the widow of Mahlon. When her mother-in-law, Naomi, returned to Bethlehem, Ruth chose to go with her. There Ruth became the wife of Boaz, a landowner of Bethlehem. A son, Obed, was born to them. Ruth was the great-grandmother of King David and is mentioned in the lineage of Jesus Christ (book of Ruth; Matthew 1:5).

S s

Samson destroys the Philistine temple (Judges 16)

sabbath (*sab*-buth): the seventh day of the week, set apart by God as a day of rest and worship. It began at sundown on Friday evening and ended on Saturday evening.

sackbut: a trombone-like instrument

sackcloth: 1. a dark coarse cloth made of goat's hair; 2. a garment made of sackcloth, probably with openings for head and arms and a slit down the front, a sash tied around the middle; usually worn by people in sorrow, and sometimes by prophets and captives

sacrifice (*sak*-ruh-fise): *v.* to give up something for someone else; to give an animal, crops, or a liquid to be burnt on an altar as an act of worship

sacrifice: *n.* 1. something that is killed or given to be burned on an altar; 2. something given up for the sake of something else

Sadducees (*sad*-yoo-seez): a religious party of the Jews in the time of Jesus. They differed from the Pharisees in that they accepted only the written law and no traditions, they did not believe in any resurrection or life after death, and they did not believe in angels or spirits. The Sadducees were well-educated aristocrats.

saint: 1. someone who is holy or set apart; 2. another name for a Christian

saith (seth): said

Salamis (*sal*-uh-mis): an important seaport and commercial center on the east cost of the island of Cyprus. It had a great limestone forum about 750 by 180 feet, which was surrounded with shops. A temple to Zeus was at the southern end. Paul and Barnabas stopped here on their first missionary journey (Acts 13:3-5).

Salmon (*sal*-mun): a man of Judah; father of Boaz, who was the husband of Ruth; great-great-grandfather of David (Ruth 4:18-22)

Salmone (sal-*mo*-nee): a cape or bluff on the eastern tip of Crete. Paul and his companions sailed by this point trying to find protection from the strong Aegean winds (Acts 27:7).

Salome (suh-*lo*-mee): 1. wife of Zebedee; mother of James and John. She was a witness to the crucifixion, and she went to the tomb of Jesus on resurrection morning (Mark 15:40, 41; 16:1); 2. the daughter of Herodias. She asked for the head of John the Baptist after dancing for Herod Antipas (Matthew 14:3-11; Mark 6:17-28).

Salt Sea; see **Dead Sea**

salutation (sal-yoo-*tay*-shun): 1. an expression of greeting or good will; 2. the words of greeting that come at the beginning of a letter

salvation (sal-*vay*-shun): 1. being saved from sin and from the punishment for sin; 2. the means of being saved

Samaria (suh-*mair*-ee-uh): 1. the capital city of the ten northern tribes of Israel. The city was built by Omri, king of Israel, on a hill about 5½ miles northwest of Shechem in the midst of a fertile valley (1 Kings 16:24). Through this valley ran the main road from Jerusalem to Galilee. The city was noted for its idolatry (1 Kings 16:32;

18:19); 2. the territory occupied by the ten tribes, or the kingdom of Israel (1 Kings 13:32; 2 Kings 17:24); 3. in NT times, Samaria was the middle province of Palestine with Galilee on the north and Judea on the south. It extended from the Mediterranean Sea to the Jordan River. When Jews traveled between Galilee and Judea, they bypassed the province of Samaria. Jesus, however, passed through Samaria (John 4:4-43; Luke 17:11). Later, when Jews were scattered from Jerusalem by the persecution of Saul, Philip and others preached about Jesus in Samaria (Acts 8:1-13; 9:31; 15:3).

Samaritans (suh-*mair*-uh-tunz): people who lived in the province of Samaria. They were part Jewish and part Gentile, resulting from mixed marriages after the fall of the northern kingdom in 721 B.C. In NT times the Jews would have nothing to do with the Samaritans (John 4:9, 20, 40).

Samothrace (*sam*-oh-thraiss): a small mountainous island in the northeast Aegean Sea off the coast of Thrace in northern Greece. Paul stopped there on his way from Troas to Neapolis (Acts 16:11).

Samson: the son of Manoah, from the tribe of Dan. He judged Israel for 20 years. He was a Nazarite, which meant he was not allowed to cut his hair or use strong drink. He was betrayed to his enemies by a Philistine woman named Delilah. Samson is remembered for his great strength, which he used against the Philistines (Judges 13—16).

Samuel: the last judge of Israel. His parents were Elkanah and Hannah. Hannah dedicated Samuel to God; when he was very young, she took him to the tabernacle. He stayed there and served the priest, Eli (1 Samuel 3). Samuel was also a prophet. After Eli's death, he was the chief religious leader in the land. He anointed Saul to be the first king of Israel (1 Samuel 10), and David to be the second (1 Samuel 16).

Sanballat (san-*bal*-lut): a very influential Samaritan. He was greatly opposed to Nehemiah's plan to rebuild the walls of Jerusalem and tried to stop him (Nehemiah 4:1-9; 6:1-14).

sanctify (*sank*-tih-fye): 1. to set something or someone apart for a sacred purpose; 2. to make holy—n. **sanctification**

sanctuary (*sank*-chuh-wer-ee): 1. a place set aside for the worship of God; 2. a place of safety or refuge.

Sanhedrin (*san*-hed-run, or san-*heed*-run): the highest Jewish council, begun after the Jews returned from Babylonian captivity. The council was made up of seventy-one men—Pharisees, Sadducees, priests, and scribes. It was led by the high priest and had power in religious and civil matters.

Sapphira (suh-*fye*-ruh): wife of Ananias. She and her husband lied about their offering to the church and were struck dead (Acts 5:1-11).

sapphire (*saf*-fier): a transparent blue precious stone

Sarah, Sarai: Her name was Sarai until God changed it to Sarah, which means "Princess." She was the wife of Abraham and came with him from Ur of the Chaldees to Canaan (Genesis 12:1-5). Her only child was Isaac, a son God promised to her in her old age (Genesis 17:15-19; 21:1-7). Through him she was the mother of the Hebrews.

sardonyx (sar-*dahn*-iks): a red-orange precious stone

Satan: a name given to the devil

Saul: 1. son of Kish, of the tribe of Benjamin. He was a handsome young man, head and shoulders taller than any of the people (1 Samuel 9:1, 2). He was anointed king by Samuel (1 Samuel 10:1). The Israelites accepted him as their king (1 Samuel 10:17-27). He defeated Israel's enemies (1 Samuel 11—14). Saul disobeyed God and because of this, his sons could not become king (1 Samuel 13). He was jealous of David and tried to kill him (1 Samuel 16—26). He took his own life with his sword after he was injured in battle (1 Samuel 31:1-4); 2. Saul, whom God called to be His apostle; see **Paul**

savior, saviour: 1. one who delivers or saves from danger and evil; 2. a name given to Jesus Christ

savor, savour: to taste; in the NT used with the meaning, "to learn, understand, perceive"—*adj.* **savory**

scapegoat: 1. one who bears the blame for others; 2. the goat that was sent by the priest into the wilderness each year, symbolically bearing the sins of the people

sceptre

sceptre, scepter (*sep*-ter): a rod held by a king as a sign of his authority

scoffer: one who mocks or makes fun of another

score: *n.* twenty

scorn: to despise, reject, or treat something with contempt, because one thinks it is beneath him

scorpion: 1. a whip with sharp points of metal at the ends to make the beating more severe; 2. a small animal like a spider, having eight legs, two claws, and a poisonous sting in its long jointed tail

scourge (skurj): *n.* a whip with pieces of bone and metal in the ends

scourge

scourge: *v.* to beat brutally by whipping

scribe; 1. a learned man of Israel who made copies of the Scriptures; 2. a secretary; 3. a teacher of the law

scrip: a small bag fastened to the waist, used by shepherds and travelers

Scripture(s): literally, "a writing;" the Bible or any part of it

scroll: a long strip of parchment containing writing, rolled on a stick at each end

Scythopolis (sye-*thahp*-oh-lis): see **Beth-shan**

seal: 1. to close tightly; 2. to fix something so that it cannot be opened without showing that it has been tampered with; 3. to make a document official by printing the official design of the king on it

sedition (seh-*dih*-shun): inciting a rebellion against the law or against the government

seduce: to lead someone astray by offering (sometimes falsely) something he wants; to tempt; to lure

seed: 1. children, descendants; 2. that from which vegetables, flowers, and other plants grow

seek: 1. to look for; to go in search of something; 2. to try to get something; *past tense,* **sought**

seer (see-ur): a prophet

seeth (*see*-eth): sees

Seir (*see*-er): see **Edom**

selah (*see*-luh or see-*lah*): a word used in the book of Psalms, thought to have meant a pause when the psalms were sung

Seleucia (sih-*loo*-shee-uh): a city built about 300 B.C. to provide a seaport for Antioch of Syria, which was about 16 miles inland. Paul and Barnabas departed from Seleucia when they started on their first missionary journey (Acts 13:4).

Sennacherib (sen-*ak*-uh-rib): a son of Sargon. He succeeded to the Assyrian throne on the death of his father about 705 B.C. He invaded Judah during the reign of Hezekiah. Jerusalem was saved by an angel who destroyed Sennacherib's entire army of 185,000 men in one night (2 Kings 18, 19; 2 Chronicles 32).

Septuagint (sep-*tyoo*-uh-jint): ancient translation of the Hebrew OT into Greek

sepulchre, sepulcher (*sep*-ul-ker): a place for putting persons who have died; a tomb. Caves were sometimes used as sepulchres, and a large stone would be placed over the opening. Sepulchres were often whitewashed not only for cleanliness and beauty, but so they could be seen easily and not touched.

Seraiah (se-*ray*-yuh, se-*rye*-uh): 1. a scribe under David (2 Samuel 8:17); 2. one of the men sent to arrest Jeremiah and Baruch (Jeremiah 36:26); 3. the high priest when Nebuchadnezzar captured Jerusalem. He was put to death at Riblah (2 Kings 25:18-21; Jeremiah 52:24-27).

seraphim (*sair*-uh-fim): six-winged heavenly beings that were seen in a vision by the prophet Isaiah before the throne of God

Sergius Paulus (*ser*-jus *pahl*-us): the proconsul, or deputy, of Cyprus when Paul and Barnabas made their first missionary journey. When he saw Paul doing the work of the Lord, he believed (Acts 13:7-12).

serpent: a snake

Seth: a son of Adam and Eve, born after the murder of Abel (Genesis 4:25, 26)

sevenfold: seven times as great or as many

Shadrach (*shad*-rak): the Babylonian name given to Hananiah, one of the Jewish young men who were taken captive to Babylon. With the help of God, he escaped death in the fiery furnace (Daniel 1:7; 3:13-30).

Shalmaneser (shal-mun-*ee*-zer): the name of several Assyrian kings. One invaded Israel during the reign of Hoshea and began the destruction of Samaria (2 Kings 17:4-6; 18:9-11).

Shamgar: a judge of Israel, son of Anath. He saved Israel by killing 600 Philistines with an oxgoad (Judges 3:31).

Shaphan (*shay*-fun): a scribe during the reign of Josiah, king of Judah. He was overseer of the finances for repairing the temple. He read the newly found book of law to the king (2 Kings 22; 2 Chronicles 34).

shalt: shall

sheaf: stalks of grain tied together in a bundle—*pl.* **sheaves**

sheaves

Shechem (*shee*-kum): a walled city in the hill country of Ephraim, about 41 miles north of Jerusalem. It was situated in the upland valley bounded on the north by Mount Ebal and on the south by Mount Gerizim. It was at the junction of important roads. Shechem was the first place visited by Abram (Genesis 12:6, 7; here spelled *Sichem*). On his return from Padan-aram, Jacob bought a piece of land at Shechem where, much later, Joseph was buried (Genesis 33:18-20; Joshua 24:32). At this place, Joshua delivered his farewell message to the tribes (Joshua 24:1, 25).

shed: 1. to throw off or let fall; 2. to cause blood to flow by cutting or wounding

shekel (*shek*-ul): for the Jews of Jesus' day, a unit of weight or a unit of money

Shem: one of Noah's three sons. At the time of the flood Shem was 98 years old and married, but had no children. He and his wife were in the ark. From him are descended the Hebrew people (Genesis 10:21; 11:10).

shepherd: a person who takes care of sheep

shew, sheweth: show, shows

shewbread (*sho*-bred): bread made without leaven and placed on a special table in the tabernacle (later, the temple). The twelve loaves of shewbread, one for each tribe, were changed each Sabbath, the old bread being eaten by the priests. It was a reminder of the bread eaten by the Israelites during the exodus from Egypt and the wanderings in the wilderness. Literally, "bread of presence."

Shiloh (*shy*-lo): a town in Ephraim on the east side of the highway connecting Shechem and Bethel (Judges 21:19). There Joshua led the Israelites to set up the tabernacle (Joshua 18:1). The tabernacle remained in Shiloh from the days of Joshua to the days of Samuel (Judges 21:19; 1 Samuel 4:3). Shiloh served as the spiritual center of Israel before Jerusalem was occupied. Samuel spent his boyhood there under the training of Eli the priest (1 Samuel 1:3, 11, 20, 28).

Shinar (shy-nahr): The land of Shinar was the plain lying between the Tigris and the Euphrates rivers, more commonly known as Babylonia in ancient times. It was the land where the city and tower of Babel were built (Genesis 11:2-9). When Nebuchadnezzar conquered Jerusalem, he took treasures from the temple to Shinar (Daniel 1:2).

shittim wood: wood from the shittah or acacia tree. This wood was used to make the ark of the covenant as well as other parts of the tabernacle. The wood is a beautiful hard wood that darkens with age.

Shur: The wilderness or desert region of Shur was south of Palestine and east of Egypt. It was in this region that Hagar wandered when she fled from Sarah (Genesis 16:7-14). After the Israelites crossed the Red Sea, they journeyed through the wilderness of Shur for three days before turning south to the Sinai peninsula (Exodus 15:22).

Shushan, Susa (shoo-shan): a capital city in southwest Persia, located about 150 miles north of the Persian Gulf. Persian kings had residences in this city. Here Daniel had the vision mentioned in Daniel 8. In Shushan, Nehemiah served as cupbearer to King Artaxerxes (Nehemiah 1:1). Queen Esther and King Xerxes (Ahasuerus) lived there (Esther 2:5-7). Many Jews lived there, and held important positions in the affairs of the city, as told in the books of Esther and Nehemiah.

Sichem, Sychem (sye-kum): see **Shechem**

Sidon (sye-don): an ancient Phoenician or Canaanite seaport on the Mediterranean coast about 22 miles north of Tyre. It was a center of trade, and filled with idolatry. Jesus visited Sidon, which was about 50 miles from Nazareth (Matthew 15:21; Mark 7:24-31). There He healed a Syrophoenician woman's daughter. People from Sidon came to Galilee to hear Jesus (Mark 3:8; Luke 6:17). On his way to Rome, Paul stopped at Sidon briefly (Acts 27:3). (Spelled *Zidon* in the OT)

sign: 1. signal; token; 2. miracle; a wonderful event that is supposed to show the presence or the will of God

signet

signet: an emblem or seal of royal authority

Silas (sye-lus): a leader in the church in Jerusalem (Acts 15:22). He traveled with Paul on his second missionary journey (Acts 15:40). They were in prison together in Philippi (Acts 16:19-40), and in the riot in Thessalonica (Acts 17:4). In Paul's letters, Silas is referred to by his Roman name, Silvanus.

Silvanus (sil-vay-nus): see **Silas**

Simeon (sim-ee-un): 1. second son of Jacob, by Leah (Genesis 29:33). He was the founder of one of the 12 tribes of

Israel; 2. the devout Jew who recognized the baby Jesus as the Messiah when Mary and Joseph brought Him for His presentation in the temple (Luke 2:25-35); 3. a Christian teacher or prophet in the church at Antioch. He was surnamed Niger, meaning black, probably because of his dark hair and swarthy complexion. He was one of the church leaders who set apart Paul and Barnabas for their first missionary journey (Acts 13:1, 2).

Simon: 1. Simon Peter, see **Peter**; 2. Simon Zelotes, one of the 12 apostles. He was a member of a party called the Zealots (Luke 6:15; Acts 1:13); 3. a brother of Jesus (Matthew 13:55); 4. a Pharisee in whose home Jesus once ate. A sinful woman anointed the feet of Jesus there (Luke 7:36-50); 5. a leper who lived in Bethany. While Jesus was in his house, Mary, the sister of Lazarus, anointed Jesus' head with precious ointment (Matthew 26:6-13; Mark 14:3-9; John 12:1-8); 6. father of Judas Iscariot (John 6:71); 7. a man from Cyrene, who was made to carry the cross of Jesus (Matthew 27:32). 8. Simon Magus, a sorcerer at Samaria who was severely rebuked by Peter (Acts 8:9-24); 9. a tanner in Joppa, at whose house Peter stayed many days (Acts 9:43; 10:6, 17, 32)

sin: disobeying any rule or law of God; refusing to do what is right; wrongdoing of any kind

Sin, wilderness of: the desert region where the Israelites journeyed on their way from Elim and the Red Sea to Mount Sinai (Exodus 16:1, 17:1; Numbers 33:11, 12)

Sinai (*sye-nye, sye-nay-ee*): 1. the Sinai peninsula is in the shape of a triangle lying between the two arms of the Red Sea. The Gulf of Suez is on the west and the Gulf of Aqaba on the east. The west shore is about 180 miles long, the east shore about 130 miles, and the north border line about 130 miles. The northern part of the peninsula is desert, and the southern part is rugged mountains. The base of the upside-down triangle separates Palestine and Egypt; 2. Mount Sinai, or Horeb as it is sometimes called, was located in the southern part of the peninsula. On this mountain Moses received the Ten Commandments, and at its base the Israelites made a covenant with God (Exodus 19—24).

sinner: 1. a wicked person; 2. anyone that commits a sin

Sisera (*sis-er-uh*): a captain in the army of Jabin, king of Hazor. He was defeated in a battle with Israel, whose army was led by Barak and Deborah. Sisera was killed by a woman named Jael (Judges 4).

slander: to insult; to make false statements against another

slay: to kill; murder—*past tense*, **slew**

sling: a long strip of leather that was wider in the middle so that a stone could be fitted into it. The sling was whirled around, then one end of the sling was released, throwing the stone with great force.

slothful: lazy

smite: 1. to kill; 2. to strike or hit hard

sobriety (so-*bry*-uh-tee): the state of being serious-minded or sober; not drunk

sod: to boil

sodden: boiled

Sodom (*sahd*-um): one of the cities in the plain or valley of the Jordan River. It was probably located at the south end of the Dead Sea. It was chosen by Lot for his home, even though Sodom was a very sinful city (Genesis 13:1-13). Later God destroyed Sodom with fire and brimstone as a punishment for its wickedness. Lot and his two daughters were spared (Genesis 19:1-29).

sojourn (*so*-jern): to stay or live in one place temporarily

Solomon: born in Jerusalem, the second son of David and Bathsheba (2 Samuel 12:24). He was the third and last king of united Israel. He ruled the most powerful nation at that time. After he worshiped and sacrificed at Gibeon, God appeared to him in a dream and told him to ask for anything he wanted. Solomon asked for an under-standing heart. God granted his wish and gave him riches and honor also (1 Kings 3:5-15). During his reign the beautiful temple in Jerusalem was built. A description of the building is found in 1 Kings 6. Solomon made two serious mistakes: he married many women for political connections with other countries, and he allowed his wives to persuade him to build temples for their heathen gods (1 Kings 11:1-8). Solomon reigned forty years. He was a writer, credited with 3,000 proverbs and 1,005 songs, including Song of Solomon, Proverbs, Ecclesiastes, and Psalms 72 and 127.

soothsayer: one who claimed to be able to foretell the future, and who earned money by predicting what would happen

sop: a piece of bread used to dip into a dish of meat and broth

Sopater (*so*-puh-ter): a Christian from Berea who, on Paul's third missionary journey, traveled with the apostle from Greece to the province of Asia (Acts 20:4)

sorcerer (*sorss*-uh-rer): a person that claimed to have magic powers and knowledge

Sosthenes (*sahs*-then-eez): a chief ruler of the synagogue in Corinth. He was beaten by a mob of angry Jews who had become upset by Paul's preaching (Acts 18:12-17).

Jesus teaches in the synagogue (Luke 4)

soul: the part of a person that thinks, feels, and causes him to act; the body is the part of a person that can be seen, while the soul is the part that cannot be seen but will live forever

sow (so): *v.* to plant seeds

sow (sow): *n.* a female pig

spake: spoke

spikenard: (*spike*-nerd): a very fragrant, expensive ointment made from an east Indian plant

spirit: not flesh; the Hebrew word means "breath" or "wind;" sometimes used to mean the same as *soul*, sometimes means the part of man that communicates with God, or a heavenly being without a body

spoil: loot; plunder taken by robbing or in time of war

staff: a heavy stick, five or six feet long, sometimes having a crook or curve at one end. Shepherds used a staff to handle the sheep, for protection, and for walking. A staff was also used by travelers.

stature (*stach*-er): 1. a person's height; 2. quality that is gained by growth or development

statute (*stach*-oot): law; commandment

stave: a rod or staff used for a weapon

steadfast: 1. not changing or moving; 2. firm in belief; faithful

Stephen: one of the first seven deacons

elected by the church in Jerusalem (Acts 6:1-6). Some leaders of the synagogue did not agree with the preaching of Stephen. They falsely accused him of blasphemy against God and condemned him to death by stoning (Acts 6:8—7:60). Stephen was the first Christian martyr. Paul was a witness to his death (Acts 8:1).

steward (*styoo*-urd): one who takes care of another's business or looks after his belongings

stocks: a wooden frame in which the feet of a prisoner were fastened (and sometimes the hands and neck)

stoning: a way the Jews punished someone when the death sentence was given; stones were thrown at the person until he died

stranger: a foreigner; one who has come from another place

stricken: afflicted by a disease, accident, or misfortune

strife: fighting; conflict between two people or groups of people

strive: 1. to struggle against something; 2. to attempt or try to do something

stubble: 1. straw; the stubs of plants left in the ground after the rest has been harvested; 2. short bristly hair or beard

stumblingblock: 1. an obstacle that might cause one to stumble; 2. something that gets in the way of unbelief or understanding

subjection (sub-*jek*-shun): the state of being under someone else's control

substance (*sub*-stunss): the real, true, or essential part of something

subtil, subtile: see **subtle**

subtle (*suh*-tul): 1. sly; crafty; tricky; 2. delicate; elusive

suffer: 1. to endure great pain or hardship; 2. to allow or permit

sundry: various; many

superscription: something written or engraved on the surface of, outside, or above something else

superscription

supplication: 1. a humble prayer; 2. a request

surety: a guarantee; an assurance; being certain

surname (*sur*-name): 1. an added name or second name that comes from a person's job, relatives, or the place he is from; 2. a name shared by all the members of a family

surpass (sur-*pass*): to exceed; to do better than another

Susannah: one of the women who provided for Jesus out of her own money (Luke 8:3)

swaddling clothes: strips of linen cloth that were wrapped around a baby

swear: 1. to make a solemn promise; 2. to make a serious statement calling upon God to witness to the truth of what one says; 3. to bind by an oath; to require to promise; 4. to use God's name in a wrong way; to curse; to use profane language

swine: pigs; hogs

Sychar (sye-kar): a town of Samaria, near Jacob's well. It was on the main road from Jerusalem, through Samaria, and on to Galilee. It was probably on the east slope of Mount Ebal and about two miles from Shechem. Jesus talked to a Samaritan woman at Jacob's well near Sychar (John 4:3-42).

synagogue (sin-uh-gahg): 1. meeting place of Jewish worshipers in NT times and later; 2. congregation of Jewish worshipers

Syntyche (sin-tih-kee): a woman in the church at Philippi. Paul begged her and Euodias to settle their differences and agree together in the Lord (Philippians 4:2).

Syracuse (seer-uh-kyoos): a seaport on the east coast of Sicily. The Alexandrian ship carrying Paul to Rome lay in the harbor at Syracuse for three days waiting for favorable winds (Acts 28:12).

Syria (seer-ee-uh): a region along the east Mediterranean coast north of Palestine. In NT times, Syria was a Roman province and ruled by a Roman governor who lived in Antioch (Acts 11:26). Paul was converted in Damascus (Acts 9:1-18); Paul and Barnabas were set apart by the church in Antioch to preach the gospel (Acts 13:1-3). Both cities were in Syria.

Tt

Jesus appears to Thomas (John 20)

tabernacle (*tab*-er-nak-ul): 1. a tent; 2. a large tent used as a place of worship for the Israelites after they had left Egypt, until the temple was built in Solomon's time. The tabernacle was 45 ft. long and 15 ft. wide and high. It was divided into the Holy Place and the Most Holy Place. The walls were made of wood and covered with gold. The entire structure was covered with layers of cloth and animal skins. The tabernacle was surrounded by a courtyard 50 ft. wide and 150 ft. long. In front of the tent was the altar of burnt offering and the laver. The entire structure and all its furnishings could be taken apart and moved as the Israelites traveled through the wilderness.

Tabernacles, feast of (or feast of Booths, feast of Ingathering): This important feast marked the end of the harvest and also served as a reminder to the Jews of their wanderings in the wilderness after they left Egypt. Each family built a small shelter or booth of branches to live in during the eight-day feast (see chart, p. 44).

Tabitha: see **Dorcas**

table of shewbread: a table three ft. long, 1½ ft. wide, and 2¼ ft. high,

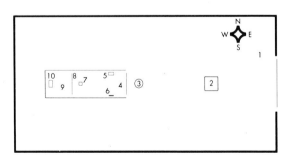

Plan of the Tabernacle

1. Courtyard
2. Altar of Burnt Offering
3. Laver
4. Holy Place
5. Table of Shewbread
6. Golden Candle-stick
7. Altar of Incense
8. Veil or Curtain
9. Most Holy Place
10. Ark of the Covenant

that stood on the north side of the Holy Place of the tabernacle. The table was made of wood and covered with gold. Golden rings with gold-covered poles enabled the table to be carried. Twelve loaves of shewbread were kept on the table.

tablet: a surface on which one could write; stone tablets were often used

Tabor (*tay*-ber): a dome-shaped mountain in Galilee on the boundary of Issachar, about 12 miles north of Mount Gilboa, and about six miles southeast of Nazareth. On the slopes of Mount Tabor Barak gathered 10,000 Israelite soldiers to fight against Sisera (Judges 4).

talent: 1. a valuable coin; 2. a unit of weight

Tamar (*tay*-mer): beautiful daughter of David and sister of Absalom (2 Samuel 13:1)

tares: weeds that resembled wheat

tarry: to wait or stay; to delay

Tarshish: It is believed by many scholars that Tarshish was a city in south Spain, near Gibraltar. Jonah planned to flee from Joppa, on the Mediterranean coast, to Tarshish when he was running away from God (Jonah 1:3).

Tarsus: the chief city of Cilicia, a province in southeast Asia Minor. It was about ten miles from the Mediterranean Sea and was famed for its schools. It was the birthplace of the apostle Paul (Acts 21:39; 22:3).

taskmaster: a boss over a work gang

Tekoa (teh-*ko*-uh): a town in Judah, about six miles south of Bethlehem, in the wilderness toward En-gedi. It was the home of Amos, the prophet (Amos 1:1).

temperance: self-control; self-restraint

tempest: a violent storm

temple: a beautiful house of worship built by Solomon and located in Jerusalem. The lavish building took seven years to complete, and was the most magnificent building ever built at that time. It was made of limestone, with cedar paneling covered with gold. The temple was patterned after the tabernacle, but was much larger. The temple contained ten golden lampstands, ten tables of shewbread, an altar of incense, and the original ark of the covenant. In the courtyard was a huge brass laver, called the brazen sea, and the altar of burnt offering, which was probably on the very rock on which Abraham was ready to sacrifice his son, Isaac, hundreds of years earlier. The temple was dedicated in about 950 B.C., and was destroyed by the Babylonians in 586 B.C. When the Jews returned from Babylon, a second temple was built, but on a smaller scale. It stood for 500 years. Herod the Great built a third temple. It was started about 20 B.C. and was not completed until shortly before A.D. 70, when it was destroyed by the Romans.

tempt: 1. to lure or entice someone to do wrong with the promise of pleasure or gain; 2. to make trial of someone; to test someone—*n.* **temptation**

Terah (*tee*-ruh): father of Abraham, Nahor, and Haran. He lived in Ur of the Chaldees most of his life. He worshiped idols. When God called Abram out of Ur, Terah went as far as Haran in Mesopotamia. There he died at the age of 205 (Genesis 11:25-32; Joshua 24:2).

testament (*tes*-tuh-ment): 1. a covenant or promise; an agreement; 2. the two main parts into which the Bible is divided

testator (*tes*-tait-er): one who leaves a covenant or will in force at his death

testify: 1. to make a statement based on personal knowledge; 2. to express a personal belief or conviction—*n.* **testimony**

tetrarch (*teh*-trark): a ruler of a fourth part of a kingdom or province; although the Bible sometimes refers to a tetrarch as a "king," he did not have as much authority as a king does

Thaddeus (*thad*-dee-us): one of the 12 apostles (Matthew 10:3; Mark 3:18); identical with Judas, not Iscariot (Luke 6:16; John 14:22; Acts 1:13), and Lebbaeus (Matthew 10:3)

thee: you

Theophilus (thee-*ahf*-uh-lus): a Christian of some prominence to whom Luke addressed the Gospel of Luke and the book of Acts (Luke 1:3; Acts 1:1)

Thessalonica (thess-uh-lo-*nye*-kuh): an ancient city in Macedonia first known as Therma. Paul preached in a synagogue there (Acts 17:1-9). To the Christians at Thessalonica Paul wrote two letters, which are found in the NT

thine: yours

Thomas: one of the twelve apostles also called Didymus, which means "twin" (Matthew 10:3; John 11:16). Thomas was not with the other apostles when Jesus first appeared to them after the resurrection. He would not believe Jesus was alive unless he saw the wounds in the hands and side of Jesus. Later Jesus appeared to all the apostles. Then Thomas believed (John 20:29). He was in the upper room on the Day of Pentecost (Acts 1:13).

thou: you

threescore: sixty

Three Taverns: see **Appii Forum**

threshing: the act of separating the grain from the chaff; winnowing

thrice: three times

thy: your

Thyatira (*thy*-uh-*tye*-ruh): a city in Asia Minor, near the boundary of Mysia. It was on the road from Pergamum to Sardis. Lydia, the seller of purple in Philippi, came from Thyatira (Acts 16:14).

Tiberias (tye-*bih*-ree-us): a city built by Herod Antipas, about A.D. 16-22. It was on the west shore of the Sea of Galilee, and named after the Roman emperor at that time, Tiberius.

Tiberias, Sea of: see **Galilee, Sea of**

Tiberius Caesar (tye-*bih*-ree-us): see **Caesar**

tidings: news; a message

Tiglath-Pileser (*tig*-lath—puh-*lee*-zer): a powerful Assyrian king. He invaded Israel during the reign of Pekah and captured several northern cities (2 Kings 15:29).

Tigris (*tye*-gris): a river in southwest Asia. It rises in the Taurus mountains and flows 1,150 miles southeast before it joins the Euphrates River. The combined rivers empty into the Persian Gulf. The Tigris is mentioned with the Euphrates and two others as rivers that watered the Garden of Eden (Genesis 2:14; Tigris is the same as *Hiddekel*).

till: to plow the soil to grow crops—n. **tiller**

Timothy: a young companion and helper of the apostle Paul (2 Timothy 4:9, 21). He lived in either Lystra or Derbe. His father was a Gentile and his mother a Jewess (Acts 20:4; 16:1; 2 Timothy 1:5). From early childhood he was instructed in the Scriptures by his mother, Eunice, and his grandmother, Lois (2 Timothy 1:5). He apparently was a convert of Paul on his first missionary journey. Timothy traveled with Paul on most of his second and third journeys. Paul wrote two letters of instruction and advice to Timothy; they are found in the NT.

tithe: *n.* a tenth part of something

tithe: *v.* to give one-tenth of an amount, especially to God

Titus: a convert and helper of Paul (Titus 1:4). He was a Greek, a son of Gentile parents (Galatians 2:3). During Paul's third missionary journey he sent Titus to Corinth to handle some problems there (2 Corinthians 2:13; 7:5-16). Titus was later left in Crete to guide the organization of the churches in that island. Paul wrote him a letter to instruct and give advice for this difficult work.

Tobiah (to-*bye*-uh): an Ammonite servant. He joined Sanballat in ridiculing Nehemiah and the Jews for rebuilding the walls of Jerusalem (Nehemiah 2:10, 19; 4:1-6; 6:1-14).

token (*to*-ken): a sign, symbol, or emblem

topaz (*to*-paz): a yellow precious stone

torment: torture; extreme pain and agony

transfiguration: 1. a change in form or appearance; 2. a name given to an event in Jesus' life in which His heavenly glory was revealed to Peter, James, and John as He talked with Moses and Elijah on a mountaintop

transgress: to sin; to break the law—n. **transgression**

translate: 1. to change; to move; to transfer; 2. to turn a message from one language into another

travail (truh-*vail*): hard labor, usually with pain

trespass: to do wrong

trial: 1. a test; 2. the act of finding out, before a judge, whether a person has actually done a wrong thing he has been accused of doing

tribe: a group of people with a common ancestor

tribulation (trib-yoo-*lay*-shun): trouble; suffering that results from persecution

tribute (*trib*-yoot): the taxes the Jews paid to Rome and to the temple

Troas (*tro*-az): a seaport in the province of Mysia in northwest Asia Minor. Paul visited Troas on various occasions (Acts 16:6-10; 20:6-12, 2 Corinthians 2:12, 13).

Trophimus (*trahf*-ih-mus): a Gentile Christian of Ephesus who was with Paul for a time on his missionary journeys (Acts 20:4; 21:29)

try: 1. to examine or test something; 2. to attempt

tumult (*too*-mult): 1. uproar and confusion in a crowd; riot; 2. violent disturbance of mind or feelings

tutor: teacher

twain: two

Tychicus (*tik*-ih-kus): a Christian from Asia who was a close friend and helper of Paul (Acts 20:4). He carried some of Paul's letters (Ephesians 6:21; Colossians 4:7).

Tyre: an ancient Phoenician city on the Mediterranean coast about twenty miles south of Sidon. Hiram, king of Tyre, provided materials for David to build his palace (2 Samuel 5:11; 1 Chronicles 14:1) and for Solomon to build the temple (1 Kings 5:1-12; 2 Chronicles 2:3-16). Jesus visited in the vicinity of Tyre and Sidon (Mark 7:24-31). On his third missionary journey, Paul stopped in Tyre for a week (Acts 21:3-7).

Ur of the Chaldees

U u

unclean: dirty or impure. The Israelites were commanded by God to avoid unclean things, such as certain kinds of food, dead bodies, or people with certain kinds of diseases.

unfeigned (un-faind): not pretended; true and honest; sincere

unity: the condition of being together as one

unleavened (un-*lev*-und): 1. without yeast or any other substance that causes dough to rise; 2. pure; uncontaminated

Ur: a leading city of Sumer (later Babylonia, which was finally occupied by the Chaldeans). It was the home of Terah and Abram (Genesis 11:31, here called Ur of the Chaldees). Education was well-developed at Ur. There was much sea trade carried on by way of the Persian Gulf.

Uriah (yoo-rye-uh): a Hittite, the husband of Bathsheba (2 Samuel 11:3). In order for David to marry the beautiful Bathsheba, he had Uriah sent to the front line of battle, where he was killed (2 Samuel 11:22-27).

Urim and Thummim (*yoor*-um, *thum*-um): literally, lights and perfections. Objects, not described by the Bible, that were part of the equipment of the high priest. These objects, perhaps precious stones, were placed in the breastplate that the high priest wore as he served the Lord. With these objects he was able to know and understand the will of God.

usurp (yoo-*serp*): to use power belonging to another; to take or use power and authority in a wrong way

usury (*yooz*-uh-ree): the lending of money with interest

uttermost: extreme; farthest away

Uzzah (uz-zuh): son of Abinadab. He was struck dead when he touched the sacred ark of the covenant to steady it as it was being moved (2 Samuel 6:3-11; 1 Chronicles 13:7-14).

Uzziah (uz-zye-uh): a king of Judah. His adviser was Zechariah, who instructed him in the way of the Lord. As long as Uzziah sought the Lord, God gave him prosperity (2 Chronicles 26:1-5). When he became proud of his success, he determined to burn incense for the Lord in the temple. This was a duty performed only by the priest. For this act, God struck Uzziah with leprosy (2 Chronicles 26:16-21).

a vineyard

vagabond: one who roams from place to place without a fixed home

vain: of no value or importance; worthless

vainglory (vain-glor-ee): pride, conceit

valor, valour (val-er): bravery; courage

vanity: 1. emptiness, futility; 2. inflated pride; conceit

Vashti (vash-tye): Queen of Persia and wife of King Xerxes. He removed Vashti from the throne and divorced her because she refused to show herself to the king's guests at a feast. Xerxes, also called Ahasuerus, then made Esther his queen (Esther 1:10—2:17).

vaunt: to boast or brag

vengeance (ven-junss): punishment in

return for a wrong act, injury, or offense

venison: the flesh of any game animal

verily: truly; of a truth

vessel: 1. a container, such as a cup, bowl, bottle, or kettle; 2. a large boat or ship

vesture: clothing, garments

vex: to annoy or disturb; to trouble

vial: a bottle or flask, a shallow bowl or basin

victuals (*vit*-tuls): food

vigilant (*vij*-uh-lent): watchful; alert; aware

vile: 1. common; of little worth; 2. foul, disgusting, or repulsive

vineyard (*vin*-yerd): a place where grapes are grown

viper: a poisonous snake

virgin: 1. a woman who has never had sexual relations with a man; 2. an unmarried woman

virtue (ver-choo): 1. power; strength; 2. goodness, or any particular kind of moral goodness; merit

vision: a kind of dream, in which God reveals himself or His will; 2. the act or power of seeing, imagining, or discerning

vow: 1. to promise; 2. to make a serious promise to God

Wise-men come to worship
(Matthew 2)

Ww

wail: to cry loudly

ward: *n.* 1. guard; 2. the state of being under guard; custody

ward: *v.* to guard or watch

wast: was

watch: an ancient division of the night-time; the Jews made three divisions; the Romans four, and the Greeks four or five

wax: to grow or increase in a particular way

welfare: well-being; health, happiness, good fortune

well-favored: good-looking; handsome

wherewithal (*wair*-with-all); 1. how; by what means; 2. with what

whither: where to; to what place, position, degree, or end

wickedness: sin; evil acts; wrongdoing

wilderness: a wasteland; a place where few people live

wiles: tricks used to lie or deceive

will: desire, command; choice

wilt: will

winepress: a place prepared for extracting juice from grapes. A large shallow vat, or container, was built above, or dug out of a rock. Grapes were placed in this upper vat, and men would trample them with their feet. The juice

winepress

would run through holes into a vat below. Then the juice would be put into containers.

winnow (*win*-oh): 1. to thresh; to separate the grain from the chaff by tossing the cut stalks of grain into the air. The seed would fall to the ground and the light straw would blow away; 2. used sometimes to mean the sweeping away of evil

winnow

wise-men: the men who traveled from the east to worship and bring gifts to the newborn King, Jesus (Matthew 2:1-12); sometimes called *Magi*

wist: know

withered: dry, shriveled, and weak

witness: *n.* one who hears or sees something and tells others about it

witness: *v.* to tell others about what you have seen or heard—see **testify**

Word of God: 1. the Bible; the Scriptures; 2. Jesus (called this in the Gospel of John)

wormwood: 1. a type of shrub whose leaves were used to make a bitter-tasting medicine; 2. something bitter or grievous

worship: to pay great respect and honor to something or someone

worthy (*wer*-thee): having enough worth; deserving

wrath: anger

wrest: 1. to twist or pull by force; 2. to gain something by force or effort

wretched (*retch*-ud): miserable; distressed; afflicted

wroth: angry

wrought: worked into shape; formed

Israel wanders in the wilderness (Exodus)

King Xerxes of Persia (Esther)

Xx

Xerxes (zerk-zeez): see **Ahasuerus**

a yoke of oxen

Yy

Yarmuk: the Yarmuk River rises in the southeast part of Mount Hermon. It flows southwest and enters the Jordan River south of the Sea of Galilee.

ye: you

yea (yay): 1. yes; 2. indeed

yield: 1. to give up; 2. to produce a certain amount

yoke: 1. a wooden bar or frame that fits across the necks of two work animals; 2. two animals yoked together

Zion

Zaccheus (zak-*kee*-us): a chief tax collector in Jericho. He was small in size, and climbed a tree to see Jesus passing by. Jesus called him down and went to his home. His life was changed when he decided to follow Jesus (Luke 19:1-10).

Zadok (*zay*-dahk): a descendant of Aaron; high priest in the time of David and Solomon. He was faithful to David through all of his troubles (2 Samuel 15:24-29; 1 Kings 1:8, 32-40).

Zarephath (*zar*-uh-fath): a Phoenician town on the Mediterranean coast. It was about eight miles south of Sidon and fourteen miles north of Tyre. At Zarephath Elijah brought a widow's son back to life (1 Kings 17:8-24).

zeal: enthusiasm; eagerness; strong feeling

Zealot (*zel*-ut): a member of a Jewish patriotic party. The Zealots hated Rome and often used violence against it.

Zebedee (*zeb*-uh-dee): a well-to-do fisherman in Galilee, the husband of Salome, and father of James and John (Mark 1:16-20, Matthew 27:56; Mark 15:40; 16:1)

Zebulun (*zeb*-yoo-lun): 1. tenth son of Jacob and sixth by Leah; 2. the tribe descended from Zebulun (Genesis 30:20; 35:23)

Zechariah (*zek*-er-*eye*-uh): 1. a man who had understanding of God and gave good advice to King Uzziah (2 Chronicles 26:5); 2. a prophet from the Babylonian captivity who returned to Jerusalem (Zechariah 1:1). He and the prophet Haggai persuaded the Jews to rebuild the temple of Jerusalem (Zechariah 8:1-9). A book of his prophecies is found in the OT; 3. in the NT, a priest, and father of John the Baptist.

He and his wife Elisabeth lived in the hill country of Judea. Elisabeth was a cousin to Mary, the mother of Jesus (Luke 1:36-40). While Zechariah was burning incense in the temple, an angel appeared and said he would have a son who would prepare the way for the coming of the Lord. Zechariah doubted this, because he and his wife were old, and he asked God for a sign. God struck him dumb until his son John was born and named (Luke 1:5-20, 57-64).

Zedekiah (zed-uh-kye-uh): a son of Josiah, and the last king of Judah. Because of the wickedness of Judah, God punished the people by allowing the Babylonian captivity. Nebuchadnezzar took Jehoiachin, king of Judah, to Babylon and made Mattaniah, whose name he changed to Zedekiah, king. Neither Zedekiah nor his people listened to the warnings of the prophet Jeremiah. Zedekiah attempted a revolt, but was defeated. His children were killed before his eyes. He was blinded and taken to Babylon in chains (2 Kings 24:15—25:7).

Zephaniah (zef-uh-nye-uh): a prophet who lived and prophesied in Judah during the reign of Josiah. The book he wrote is found in the OT

Zerubbabel (zeh-rub-uh-bul): when the king of Babylon allowed the captive Jews to return to their homeland, one of the groups was led by Zerubbabel and the high priest, Jeshua (Nehemiah 12:1-9). They restored the worship and laid the foundations of the temple. Then their work was interrupted (Ezra 4). Later the work was resumed through the encouragement of the prophets Haggai and Zechariah. A great celebration was held at the dedication when the temple was completed (Ezra 6:14-18; Haggai). This second temple is often called Zerubbabel's temple.

Ziba (zye-buh): a servant in Saul's household. He was appointed by King David to work for Jonathan's lame son, Mephibosheth (2 Samuel 9:2-9).

Zidon: see Sidon

Zilpah (zil-puh): a maidservant given by Laban to Leah at the time of her marriage to Jacob. She was the mother of Jacob's sons Gad and Asher (Genesis 29:24; 30:9-13)

Zimri (zim-rye): fifth king of the northern kingdom, Israel. His reign was short and wicked (1 Kings 16:15-20).

Zion (zye-un): a name for Jerusalem, especially the hill where the temple was; Heaven

Zipporah (zip-por-uh): daughter of Jethro, a priest in Midian. She was the wife of Moses and had two sons, Gershom and Eliezer (Exodus 2:21, 22; 18:2-4).

Zorah (zo-ruh): a town in the lowland of Judah; the home of Manoah, Samson's father (Judges 13:2). Samson was buried near there (Judges 16:31).